THE JESUS MUSIC

A **VISUAL STORY** of **REDEMPTION** As **TOLD** By **THOSE WHO LIVED IT**

THE
JESUS MUSIC

MARSHALL TERRILL

FOREWORD BY GREG LAURIE

K·LOVE
BOOKS

NASHVILLE, TENNESEE

K-LOVE Books
5700 West Oaks Blvd
Rocklin, CA 95765

Printed in the United States of America.

First edition: 2021
10 9 8 7 6 5 4 3 2 1

ISBN: 978-1-954201-12-5 (hardcover)
ISBN: 978-1-954201-13-5 (eBook)
ISBN: 978-1-954201-14-9 (audiobook)

Publisher's Cataloging-in-Publication data
Names: Terrill, Marshall, author. | Laurie, Greg, foreword author.
Title: The Jesus music : a visual story of redemption as told by those who lived it / Marshall Terrill ; foreword by Greg Laurie.
Description: includes index. | Rocklin, CA: K-LOVE Books, 2021.
Identifiers: ISBN 978-1-954201-12-5 (hardcover) | 978-1-954201-13-2 (ebook) | 978-1-954201-14-9 (audio)
Subjects: LCSH Contemporary Christian music. | Christian rock music. | Bible in music. | Popular music—Religious aspects. | Popular culture—Religious aspects—Christianity. | Jesus Christ. | Redemption. | BISAC MUSIC / Religious / Christian | MUSIC / Religious / Contemporary Christian | RELIGION / Christian Living / Personal Growth
Classification: LCC ML3187.5 .T47 2021 | DDC 242–dc23

Cover and interior design by Dexterity, in partnership with The Brain Design and Sarah Siegand.

Cover photo courtesy of LIONSGATE® and Kingdom Story Company.

I am dedicating this endeavor to my sweet and kind mother, Carolyn Jane Terrill. Without her spiritual guidance and Christian example, I would not have had the foundation to write this book.

CONTENTS

FOREWORD

It's interesting, isn't it?

It used to be that when some entrepreneurial seminary graduate wanted to "plant" a church, finding a musician to "lead" worship was an afterthought. In fact, it wasn't that long ago when a "song leader" stepped to the pulpit and waved his arms, conductor like, as parishioners sang along. Of course, there was someone plunking at the keys on an upright spinet piano with a white songbook opened to the hymn of the morning. For decades this defined "worship leading," and if you weren't sure which hymns you were singing that day, their numbers were posted at the front of the church for your convenience. There were no surprises.

Remember boards like the one above?

If there was a word that would have described Christian music back then, it would have been "predictable." A little boring. Maybe even stodgy. Oh, I'm sure these hymns had a contemporary feel to them when they were written hundreds of years ago, but today, though we appreciate their deep content and doctrinal soundness, they are not quite as impactful.

The book you're about to read chronicles a movement. A revolution, really. At first, there were a handful of courageous, believing musicians whose lives were anything but ordinary or mundane. They loved music and truly embraced the biblical mandates to sing (there are lots of these). But the stuff they were expected to sing in church didn't cut it. So much so that these daring song-makers changed the face of everything that called itself church music. Music with the prefix . . . Christian.

Sometimes these people were demonized from the pulpits proclaiming this music was "straight from hell." Parents were ordered to destroy their children's Christian record collections in the name of obedience, separation from the world, and holiness.

Undaunted by the controversy, the musicians creating this music did not go away. In fact, they proliferated . . . and their tribe grew. And did they change the face of Christian music? Yes, they did.

Were they—or the songs they wrote and performed—born of hell? No.

Quite the opposite, actually.

This book was been written to not only identify these adventurers, but to celebrate them. It was written to show that God uses sinful, ordinary people who often fall short to do extraordinary things.

People like you . . . and me.

Truly, the Bible is also brimming with the accounts of flawed people who changed the world.

Samson was a powerful judge and leader of Israel, yet he fell into sexual sin. David was the greatest King in the history of God's chosen people. He was the giant killer and the musician who wrote supernaturally inspired songs to God. We call them Psalms today. David was also a courageous warrior. But David had his fall, not on the battlefield, but in the bedroom with Bathsheba. Despite this, David is remembered as "The man after God's own heart" (1 Sam. 13:14). That is not said of any other person in the Bible.

Failures happened in the New Testament too. Who can forget Peter's outright denial of the Lord or Thomas's steadfast skepticism about the resurrection?

To all of these people, God gave a second chance. He made a message out of their messes. A testimony out of their tests. And the same is true of some of the artists in this book. Creating art and music is not an easy thing to do. Otherwise, we would all do it. It takes perseverance, discipline, and hard work.

The master artist, Michelangelo is the perfect example of this. When we think of him we remember the brilliance of his towering statue of David sculpted from a single piece of stone and, of course, his magnificent painting on the ceiling of the Sistine Chapel.

A lot of pain, sacrifice, and self-denial went into his work, though, that is unknown to most.

Michelangelo himself said, "If people knew how hard I had to work to gain my mastery, it would not seem so wonderful at all . . . If you knew how much work went into it, you wouldn't call it genius."

Not too long ago, a dean at one of the largest design colleges in the country let me in on a little secret. He told me that even though artists of every medium are often painted as aloof and celestially minded, they're actually gutsy. Daring. Often fearless. They inherently have a pioneering spirit, going where no mortal has ever dared to go.

Here's how he explained it to me: artists move into an area—sometimes all alone—and after years of blood, sweat, and tears, they create a space where others notice, tolerate, accept, embrace, then love what they've fashioned . . . so much so that the others actually want to live there.

"Developers" soon follow and build around that space. Santa Fe, New Mexico, was a backwater town until Georgia O'Keefe and Alfred Stieglitz moved there in the 1920s. Now it's a millionaire's playground. Lower Manhattan in the 1980s had affordable lofts that artists snatched up because they were cheap and the streets were seething with crime. No more. Because many were introduced to this space through artistry and then drawn in, it's not affordable anymore. And Ojai, California, was once a sleepy, nothing locale, until artisans flooded in. This area has followed the same trajectory. There, the billionaires are pushing out the millionaires.

In this book, Marshall Terrill demonstrates how Contemporary Christian music (CCM) followed this very same pattern. It went from lone hippies strumming guitars on a California beach to multi-millionaire artists flying around in private jets, enjoying mainstream success with all the trappings of a rock star. I should know. I was there when it all started.

I grew up with many of the artists profiled in this book. I witnessed their starts, their stumbles, their ascensions and, in some cases, their falls. I have seen CCM change and morph with the times and cover every possible genre there is. I've seen it go through the acoustic Southern California guitar of Jesus rock, the slick Nashville-based pop rock of the 1970s, the synth-based sounds of the 1980s, the screaming guitars sound of metal rock, rap, and alternative in the 1990s, and the return to worship at the beginning of the new millennium. Through it all, though the music changed from what it had been, the message never did. And these artists' intensity originated from the same place—a boldness, fearlessness, and an eagerness for spreading the gospel message of salvation.

In the earlier stages of Christian music, it could be somewhat derivative. A 'sanitized version' of what was popular on the music charts.

Not anymore. Christian music has clearly come into its own. Not just because of its lyrical content but because of very talented artists that have elevated it with well-crafted songs that stand on their own against the top songs in mainstream culture.

We are at a stage where in many ways, musically speaking, CCM is equal to and often surpasses what we hear on the secular charts. It is art as it was meant to be used—to glorify the one who gave it to us.

As Christians, we're fortunate. We get to hear the music and sing the lyrics. We've been lifted by the music and have come to believe the true message, and we receive the many blessings of the art and ministry.

Witnessing the start of CCM and watching it evolve has transformed the whole idea of church music that still does what those old hymns did . . . draw people in by clearly identifying the historic birth, death, and resurrection of the Savior; celebrating His love and grace; and inviting His people to lift their voices in unison. In all-out praise.

These daring homesteaders have brought pure joy and blessing to my life. My heart will forever be filled with gratitude for them. I hope this book will mean as much to you as it does to me.

Greg Laurie
Harvest Ministries

TOBYMAC PERFORMS AT THE 2010 DOVE AWARDS.

INTRODUCTION

History is a curious thing.

If you look at a timeline over centuries, there appear to be seasons when the events of humanity have plodded along without noticeable peaks or valleys—flatlines that seem to last for hundreds of years, manifold decades when nothing notable happens.

Most recorded history isn't like this. Centuries of doldrums have been changed by something as ordinary as weather . . . such as when the Spanish Armada was destroyed by a storm in the English Channel, halting a massive invasion. Sometimes changes can be born of technology, like gunpowder or penicillin or electricity or the printing press.

A student specializing in looking back at eons of the malaise realizes that individuals can change history, for better or worse: Lenin or Washington, Hitler or Jesus.

Sometimes groups of people will turn a tide, like the millions who courageously stood firm during the summer of 1989, breaking down the Berlin Wall—an Iron Curtain that had hung over eastern Europe for almost fifty years broken into shards. Europeans dared to want something else.

When the Black Death hit western Europe and a third of the population died, it hastened the end of feudal society. Peasants looked around, saw that most of their village was gone, and decided to abandon their towns. The local lord could work his own fields, thank you very much. They were going somewhere else.

The fire in enough bellies is usually why things change. When enough people decide they want something else, they move mountains. In most cases, we think in terms of wars, technological advances, and politics, but popular culture is one of the biggest influences for change in this modern era.

For decades, people tuned their dashboard AM radios to predictable religious music and preaching. But one day something unknown rushed from their paper-thin automobile speakers. It sounded something like rock 'n' roll, yet it felt strangely redemptive. Clean. Sort of like gospel music . . . but not so much.

And that's what *The Jesus Music: A Visual Story of Redemption as Told by Those Who Lived It* is about: people creating something they wanted, something that had never existed before. The people were young Christians, and what they wanted was music—good music they could listen to all week long.

Elvis and Johnny Cash had woven the gospel into 1950s rock 'n' roll. Artists like the Beatles and the Byrds incorporated spiritual concepts into pop music in the decade that followed. But those touches were stylistic flourishes. Cut it in half, and it was still secular music.

Before Christian rock, all young Christians had was church music. And, as at least one person you'll hear from in this book said, "It wasn't very good." The young people who wanted something different may have been Christians, but they were used to good music. So why wasn't there good music that praised God *and* appealed to the tastes of young people?

That was how Contemporary Christian music was born.

This book contains the story of its pioneers, prophets, saints, devils, angels, tortured souls, train wrecks, and clashes. It was a Christian genre that begat many other genres: Christian versions of heavy metal, grunge, pop, rap, and alternative. But however the message was delivered, it all pointed in one direction: to the Lord.

Author, filmmaker, evangelist, and senior pastor of Harvest Church, Greg Laurie, explained: "I think you can sum it up in one word: it's *hopeful* music. Some songs are more analytical, some talk about struggle, but ultimately, you'll find many of the songs in what we call contemporary Christian rock and what was originally called Jesus Music pointing to God in some way, shape, or form— some more overtly, some based on Scripture—but all intended to point up.

"And I think [it's] really important to have redemptive music in a culture like we have today because as you listen to other music it can be degrading. It can just bring you down. You turn it on and listen. It's dark.

"But this Christian music lifts you up and tells us a better day is coming and there's a God who loves us and there's a God who cares. I think it's a powerful force for good."

A great cathedral was designed to draw the eye heavenward, toward the glory of God. When you admired it from the outside, you gazed at the sky-piercing spire. But inside, you were drawn into the nave, stained glass soaring far above the altar. It was almost like the outside lifted your heart, but the inside inspired your soul. No one ever walked into St. Patrick's Cathedral in New York and stared at the floor.

This is a metaphor for music. For some, in settings like these great structures, even monotone Gregorian chants lift the spirit. However, harmonic voices fill the hollows with lasting echoes.

Throughout history, worthy Christian art, music, and design has been aimed at illuminating God's message by lifting, pointing up.

And that's true for visionary Christian rockers of many stripes—singers, guitar players, drummers, and even the rowdies wearing eyeliner and yellow-and-black spandex on the Sunset Strip. In this book, you'll meet some ordinary and some far-out characters. Hippies, Jesus freaks, metalheads, pop stars, punkers, rappers, alt-rockers, and some Christians who defy categorization.

But they all have the same heart, the same aim: loving Jesus and creating music . . . Jesus Music.

RANDY MATTHEWS PERFORMS AT EXPLO '72.

CHAPTER 1

GENESIS

You might not want to leave this book out where the kids can pick it up. And you definitely should think twice before giving it to your parents as a gift. Yes, this is a history of Contemporary Christian music. But while it's Christian, the main word here is music. It's a raw, uncensored, unfiltered, and sometimes nasty story about complicated people making what they believed was worthwhile music.

the known world; they sacrifice comfort, ease, and security, all on a gamble that there's something out there they can do better than anyone else. What they have is faith—faith to endure almost guaranteed hardship; faith that sometimes appears hopeless; faith that sometimes will have people questioning their sanity. People thought Noah was nuts until the rain wouldn't stop and they were sucking serious water.

GENESIS

It was in some ways a mess. But in many ways, it was beautiful.

A beautiful mess.

After all, we're talking about pioneers here. Pioneers are usually desperate people—people willing to risk it all; people willing to tackle new frontiers. No one living comfortably in a New York City brownstone ever said, "Hey, let's get rid of everything, buy a covered wagon, and go west!"

But pioneers are people who swagger into daring new ground. They travel to the fringes of

This book is filled with messy people, visionaries, prophets, madmen and madwomen, backstabbers, thieves, and cheaters—and that was just at the beginning. Wait until accountants, managers, promoters, and label execs enter the picture. And we haven't even introduced drugs, alcohol, sexual temptation, and outsized egos to the mix.

All of this got its start in the cauldron of 1960s America.

Allow me to give a brief overview of that tumultuous but wonderful decade if you weren't there; or if you were there, time and certain illegal substances might have dulled or impaired your memory. In short, nobody did anything halfway. Whether protesting the Vietnam War, marching in a civil rights protest, or lying stoned in a muddy field at Woodstock with thousands of blissed-out people, these were norms of the day. Hair couldn't be too long. Vans couldn't be too groovy. Ties were only good for headbands, and your thumb was your ticket to anywhere in the country.

"The experiment of drugs, sex, rock 'n' roll, and the arrival of the hippie lifestyle pretty much started around '66, '67 in Haight-Ashbury," said musician Tommy Coomes, founding member of Love Song. "It made its way down to Southern California pretty quickly. And around the world."

While the Vietnam War dominated headlines, the decade started off with a lot of wishful thinking.

ALL OF THIS GOT ITS START IN THE CAULDRON OF 1960s AMERICA.

President John F. Kennedy declared America's "New Frontier" would make great strides, which included sending a man to the moon and eliminating injustice, inequality, and tyranny. With his elegant and stylish wife, Jackie, at his side, along with their children, Carolyn and John, Kennedy's arrival in Washington DC was both a political and cultural moment. Fully free from the grip of World War II and the Korean conflict, the country—especially its youth—felt hopeful about the future. But an assassin's bullet found its mark in Dallas, Texas,

EXPLO '72, ALSO KNOWN AS THE "CHRISTIAN WOODSTOCK," TOOK PLACE IN DALLAS, TEXAS, AND DREW TENS OF THOUSANDS OF ATTENDEES. THE JESUS MOVEMENT OF THE EARLY 1970S WAS PART OF THE LAST GREAT AWAKENING ACCORDING TO CHRISTIAN HISTORIANS.

on November 22, 1963, violently terminating the dream. The nation was undone. Anyone alive on that day will immediately remember where they were and what they were doing when they heard the news. The relatively peaceful years of Eisenhower and Kennedy were gone. No one knew it yet, but they were mourning more than a slain president that day. The assassination was further dirtied by controversy and conspiracy theories.

Kennedy's death coincided with the Vietnam War, the civil rights movement, protests on college campuses, debates about systemic racism, and an emerging counterculture. Student activists grew more radical, hippies engaged in free love, and everyone under thirty smoked lots of dope. They followed and held up Martin Luther King Jr. and Robert Kennedy as heroes to be emulated. These peaceful figures also ended up like JFK, assassinated by extremists.

Wishful thinking was equally dead. The war intensified, growing bigger and worse every year. Planeloads of dead GIs began arriving home, but they were outnumbered by thousands more flying in the other direction across the Pacific to take their place. And how about the terrible reception these warriors received upon their return from a hideous fighting experience? Their sacrifice was met with derision, further dividing the country. Soon, the question of whether all this derision was justified was spoken out loud everywhere. The cost was impossible to ignore, however.

"My generation had seen all of the civil unrest and the craziness. Most of us were a bunch of hippies trying to escape the pain and the misery," said Glenn Kaiser, a Chicago-based Christian blues singer and founding member of the Resurrection Band (also known as REZ). They wanted "anything other than the 'status quo' of the American Dream [and] that was not an American Dream but an American Nightmare . . . this was partly why a lot of us ended up saying, 'Eat, drink, and be merry, for tomorrow we die.'"

Mirroring the war was violence at home. Some of it took place at the dinner table, where parents who wished for a return to the domestic bliss of the 1950s fought with their children who saw only injustice. By the end of the sixties, some of the hippies and radicals had had enough marching. They began bombing. In one eighteen-month period between 1971 and 1972, there were

THESE WERE INCREDIBLE TIMES, AND SO WAS THE MUSIC.

2,500 bombings—almost five per day. Churches were bombed. Campus ROTC buildings were bombed. So were federal buildings, court complexes, police headquarters, and airports. In March 1971, the radical leftist group the Weather Underground set off a device in the US Capitol to protest the US invasion of Laos. No building or entity, it appeared, was off-limits; all were fair game. Experimenting with drugs like marijuana and LSD also took a darker turn toward heroin, morphine, and speed . . . stuff that could and did cause real damage.

Cocaine entered the scene in the seventies and seemed to be the meanest of all the drugs, according to street-level experience. One rock executive in the music business said, "God gave us cocaine to let us know we were making too much money." It destroyed financial success and personal lives at an alarming rate. So did the other chemicals.

TORTURED AND DICHOTOMOUS, NORMAN'S LIFE SEEMED LIKE ONE BIG DOGFIGHT.

"My philosophy was that God had given us LSD, and if you weren't brave enough to experiment with drugs, you'd miss God because I thought that was the secret key," said Chuck Girard, a co-founding member of Love Song. "We were all taking LSD, and all of a sudden our heroes were starting to come out and tell us how they were taking LSD. So . . . we had affirmation: 'Oh, they're on our trip.' I thought the Beatles had found a deeper version of the truth."

These were incredible times, and so was the music. Truly, the best of the twentieth century. On any given day, you could hear on the radio artists such as the Beatles, Bob Dylan, Aretha Franklin, the Rolling Stones, the Beach Boys, Led Zeppelin, the Who, the Byrds, Jimi Hendrix, Cream, the Doors, Janis Joplin, Sly and the Family Stone, Jefferson Airplane . . . and let's not forget the great Motown artists and West Coast sounds of surf and folk-rock bands.

The musicians—mostly in their late teens and early twenties—held a special place in the zeitgeist of the Age of Aquarius.

"In the sixties, our heroes were like Pied Pipers. The Beatles, Jim Morrison of the Doors, Jimi Hendrix, Janis Joplin. They were the ones leading us. To use sixties vernacular, we thought they were 'turned on,'" Greg Laurie said. "Musicians of the 1960s had a great influence on the lifestyle of young people. We would actually read the notes on the back of records, looking for answers. It was a whole different time. I think we were really searching like never before. It's kind of sad really, but we were just kids."

The music was spellbinding, fun, uplifting, challenging, psychedelic, dramatic, and sometimes dark ("Eve of Destruction" by Barry McGuire, "Sympathy for the Devil" by the Rolling Stones, and "The End" by the Doors quickly come to mind). To their parents' dismay, young Christians liked it too. There was no Christian equivalent to that. All they had was the music they heard on Sundays.

Their parents had Pat Boone, Anita Bryant, Johnny Mathis, and Connie Francis. But they were about as cool as the "Wun'uhful Wun'uhful" Lawrence Welk, who once fired his champagne lady for showing too much leg on his long-running TV show.

Elvis Presley was the first to incorporate gospel into rock 'n' roll. Johnny Cash was a close second. The two Southerners, who broke through with their slicked-back hair, twangy charm, and rebel images, loved their mommas, loved their country, and were raised in the church. Their secular music sold so well that record companies waited until their artists were fully established before releasing their gospel material . . . and encouraged them to wait another few years before repeating the exercise. (Ironically, Elvis received fourteen Grammy nominations, but won only three, all for his gospel albums.)

The labels did it to appease their artists' mommas, not to sell a million albums. These were songs you were never going to hear on the radio because there was no market and no audience.

During the 1960s, rock stars, who were on a constant quest for enlightenment, sometimes needed some soul

11

THE JESUS MOVEMENT DIDN'T GO UNNOTICED BY THE PRESS,
WHO GAVE IT COVERAGE IN *ROLLING STONE*, *LIFE*, *LOOK*,
AND A 1971 COVER STORY IN *TIME* MAGAZINE.

back in their music. Artists like the Beatles ("The Inner Light"), Tommy James ("Sweet Cherry Wine"), Johnny Rivers ("Jesus Is a Soul Man"), Norman Greenbaum ("Spirit in the Sky"), and the Byrds ("Jesus Is Just Alright") incorporated a few spiritual ideas into pop music, but they were mostly metaphorical.

The Monterey Pop Festival in June 1967 kicked off the peace and love moment. It was three days of bliss and no arrests. That movement ended at Altamont with the death of four individuals. Another movement, however, was on the horizon.

It was called "Jesus Music."

For some traditionalists, the movement was only Christian by a hair. A visionary artist named Larry Norman began to change all of that.

"Larry Norman, who most people considered the father of Contemporary Christian rock, was definitely not the first person ever to play rock 'n' roll with a Christian message," said John J. Thompson, a music historian and the author of *Raised by Wolves*. "But he is certainly the first rock star in Christian rock, undeniably."

Considered by many to be the "Bob Dylan of Contemporary Christian music," in reality, Norman was the genre's John the Baptist.

But unlike John the Baptist, he didn't get his head cut off. If anybody chopped off heads, it was this guy. The Texas-born singer, songwriter, record label owner, and record producer was a force of nature. Not even the devil could stop him.

Norman was a rocker who attended an African American Pentecostal church in his youth. As a teen, his flower power band People! charted many regional singles, had a million-copy seller in the 1968 release "I Love You," and opened for or shared the bill with acts like Van Morrison, the Animals, the Doors, the Who, Janis Joplin, and Jimi Hendrix. He was an in-house writer for Capitol Records, the most prestigious music label of the era, penning musicals and rock operas during the day. At night he preached on the street to businessmen, transvestites, prostitutes, and hippies alike. But some of his rock star peccadillos died hard. He constantly fought with record label executives, waged war with the Christian church, and rarely had a good thing to say about the Contemporary Christian music industry ("Sloppy thinking, dishonest metaphors, and bad poetry"). But when it came to the ladies, he was all love . . . possibly too much of it.

In *Why Should the Devil Have All the Good Music?*, a 2018 biography of Norman, author Gregory Alan Thornbury writes that the long-haired,

LARRY NORMAN'S *UPON THIS ROCK* (1969), WAS A WATERSHED ALBUM BUT CAPITOL RECORDS EXECUTIVES WEREN'T EVEN AWARE THEY HAD A CHRISTIAN ALBUM ON THEIR HANDS.

blond singer was catnip to women. He stepped out on his wives and sang songs about heroin, sipping whiskey from a paper cup, and venereal disease to astonished parishioners.

"The early stuff he put out . . . Christian radio today, no way would they play it," said John Styll, founder and editor of *Contemporary Christian Music* magazine.

The Texan wasn't very affable, approachable, or down-home, for that matter. He was tortured and dichotomous, and his life seemed like one big dogfight. He generally refused to sign autographs and wasn't big on polite chitchat with the fans, but he had time for them if they were in need or wanted prayer. He had a string of broken relationships—romantic, professional, and longtime friendships. Norman led fellow musician and protégé, Randy Stonehill, to faith in Christ and secured for him a record deal only to steal his publishing and later marry his first wife.

Norman didn't stop there. He often antagonized his audiences, browbeat his band and crew, and had a Machiavellian history of taking advantage of people, including fellow artists and even his fans. One person who worked for Norman made the wry observation that the musician was "only a Christian on the stage."

His contradictions were endless.

"Was he a complicated character? That's putting it mildly," remarked John J. Thompson.

There were also questions about his character and challenges to his status as a follower of Christ. "Some people felt he wasn't truthful," John Styll said. "Some people felt like all the liner notes, even the ones that sort of praised him, were written by him!"

Styll painfully recalled the time when *Contemporary Christian Music* magazine placed Norman on their cover and almost regretted the move.

GREG LAURIE LEADING A WORSHIP SERVICE AT CALVARY CHAPEL IN COSTA MESA, CALIFORNIA, WITH JESUS ROCK BAND THE WAY BACKING HIM.

"Larry was a photographer and very particular about the photographs that were used, and I don't think he was happy about the selection," Styll said. "He drove down to my house in Orange County from LA where he lived. Showed up at my door at 1:30 in the morning with strips of 2x2 pictures in a loop so we could pick out a different cover—1:30 in the morning at my house! He didn't like *CCM* magazine. He sure wanted to be on the cover, though . . . He was a bit of a difficult person, a brilliant artist. A lot of brilliant artists are kinda miserable human beings. It's part of what makes them great artists."

REZ band lead singer Glenn Kaiser was also familiar with Norman's peculiarities but allowed him to go unchecked.

"I'd known Larry better than Larry probably wished I'd known Larry," Kaiser said. "I almost never confronted him because I knew other people who had. I knew he made some pretty lousy choices. So have I. So have you. So has everybody."

Whatever demons Norman had, he was supremely talented and a mesmerizing performer with admirers the likes of Bob Dylan and Bono. He sold out venues like London's Royal Albert Hall, the Hollywood Palladium, and the Sydney Opera House in Australia and played at the White House. Former Vice President Mike Pence dedicated his life to Christ at a 1978 music festival headlined by Norman. Even Paul McCartney recognized Norman's star potential, telling him, "You could be famous if you'd just drop the God stuff."

Norman was more interested in being what he saw as a pure Christian beholden to God but not the church. His 1968 conversion changed his spiritual outlook, his worldview, and of course, his music. Norman's December 1969 solo album, *Upon This Rock*, was as unforgiving as he was. The material he sang in those vinyl grooves spoke to lost souls, people waging spiritual battles, and skeptics of traditional religion. His Christian outsider status was culturally relevant and provocative.

"My dad has always believed that the secular world stole church music and turned it into rock music, rock 'n' roll," said Mike Norman, the Christian rocker's eldest son. "My dad always felt it was his mission to bring it back into the church. My dad was passionate about changing the world and he did it the only way he knew how."

Norman certainly rocked Greg Laurie's world in early 1970.

Laurie was a long-haired high school senior at Newport Beach's Harbor High when he first heard Larry Norman. Laurie was a newly minted Christian and was willing to give up his beloved rock 'n' roll if he could find faith-based music that was equivalent to what he had been reared on. He found what he was looking for inside a local coffee shop.

"It wasn't really a coffee shop, but we had coffee there. It was a place where we would gather for prayer and then we would go out and share the gospel," Laurie recalled. "They had a record player,

THE JESUS FREAKS DIDN'T WEAR TRADITIONAL CHURCH ATTIRE, AND AS IT TURNED OUT, THEY WEREN'T ABOUT TO LISTEN TO TRADITIONAL CHURCH MUSIC, EITHER. FOR THIS GENERATION, MUSIC WAS EVERYTHING.

and I was flipping through what really looked like the lamest albums of all time. I went, 'Bad, bad, bad.' As a seventeen-year-old, they appeared to me to be really dorky-looking people, trying to look cool, which is the most uncool thing you possibly could do. Then I come across this record. It says, 'Larry Norman, *Upon This Rock*.' It has this guy Larry Norman with long hair sort of reaching out. I thought, *What is this?* I placed it on the turntable, and I was blown away. Great lyrics, catchy melody, and even humorous at times. To me, that was the

first real record of what we would later call 'Jesus Music.'"

A lot of Christians felt the same way.

"Larry is the single most important figure in Contemporary Christian music," said musician Chuck Girard. "He wasn't writing songs for the church. They were very clever, very powerful songs for nonbelievers."

Upon This Rock was a watershed album (not to mention an epic anomaly) that was part of his original deal with Capitol Records. The deal he struck under executive Mike Curb gave him total artistic control to create whatever music he desired. The LP had high production value, strong songwriting, and musical hooks on par with his former rock contemporaries. Because Capitol didn't know how to market the album—or there simply was no market for it at the time—*Upon This Rock* didn't sell well.

Ken Mansfield, an executive who worked for Capitol at the time, said everybody at the label dropped the ball when it came to promoting Larry Norman, including him.

"I find it hard to admit this, but as the head of national promotion and artist relations, we paid almost no attention to Larry and his product," Mansfield said. "This probably had mostly been due to my non-Christian lifestyle at that time, and we had so many major big-selling artists to attend to, including the Beatles and the Beach Boys.

ROCK COULD BE CHRISTIAN *AND* POPULAR.

"He never stopped by to introduce himself or had a manager who sought efforts on his behalf. In fact, I am unaware we even had any viable presence, interest, or expertise in Christian music and its outlets at the time. Even worse yet, typically when any record in any format started garnering sales, I was made aware by the sales division to have my team jump on that record with extra promotional efforts in order to bring it 'home.'"

However, amazingly, the album *Upon This Rock* "jump-started a musical genre and launched a thousand imitators" according to one critic. Another called it "the *Sgt. Pepper's* of Christian rock."

Music critics and historians deemed *Upon This Rock* the first full-blown Christian rock album, a groundbreaking effort that married rock music with the gospel. For all of the accolades Norman received, there was a price to be paid for his fervor. Capitol dropped him from its roster.

But there was something bigger to be gained.

Rock could be Christian *and* popular. Larry Norman was the first to prove this. He was a true pioneer, and more change was to come.

CAPITOL RECORDS DURING THIS ERA WAS THE PREMIER RECORD LABEL AND HOME TO ARTISTS SUCH AS FRANK SINATRA, THE BEATLES, THE BEACH BOYS, AND LARRY NORMAN.

17

CHAPTER 2

PASTOR CHUCK
AND HIS MERRY BAND OF HIPPIES

Chuck Smith was a balding, married, middle-aged preacher with four kids. He was a man's man who liked pro football and baseball, taught his children respect for authority and God, and like many men of his era, believed *you worked hard for what you got and were thankful for the gifts God bestowed upon you.* He was highly competitive and for relaxation would do construction work. Smith grew up in the shadow of the

about his faith and the fate of his fellow man, but rebellious and unkempt hippies tested the bounds of his compassion.

In December 1965, he was hired to take over a dwindling congregation whose membership numbered approximately twenty-five people. It was a slight financial step-down from his previous pastorate at the Corona Christian Church in Corona, California, but he was being hamstrung by the elders

PASTOR CHUCK
AND HIS MERRY BAND OF HIPPIES

Great Depression and World War II, a time when individuals "pulled themselves up by the bootstraps" if they wanted to succeed in this world. He was a no-nonsense guy who believed in love and discipline; that marriage was between a man and a woman; that the appearance of your lawn reflected your priorities and moral character; that a belt every once in a while kept the kids in line; that shoes should shine; and that dinner was to be on the table at six sharp.

"Pastor Chuck" worked hard to provide for his family and had no use for slackers. He was serious

there and needed a new challenge. His new gig as the pastor of Calvary Chapel in Costa Mesa started offering some autonomy as well with its $135 per week salary. But there were other advantages, like access to the beach. (Smith was a big-time surfer.) The church started as a Bible study that eventually slid into a freestanding, brick-and-mortar building, then saw moderate growth under Smith's energetic leadership and conversational sermons. He felt an instant rapport with the congregation, who were mostly middle-class and conservative . . . and joyful.

According to Smith's son, his father had a "sincere love for strangers and a fearless commitment to telling anyone who crossed his path about salvation through Jesus Christ."

But he had a strong dislike for hippies. He didn't understand them. He couldn't fathom why they were so unhappy with their lives or why they chose the unconventional lifestyle they did. Smith's mindset concerning longhairs was simple: Get

of the Great Depression that put our very survival at stake. But here were these kids, flaunting their rejection of the very things we worked hard to earn. Their behavior was unbelievable. Outrageous."

While his wife, Kay, agreed with Chuck in theory, she was fascinated with these slightly dazed "flower children." Kay was curious by nature and a true people person. Her heart was filled with love and compassion for others. One day while driving,

a bath, get a job, get a life. It goes without saying he probably thought a haircut was needed as well. He could not grasp the disenfranchised hippie counterculture that had emerged in the late sixties, rebelling against anything or anyone who smacked of middle-class or higher . . . or whatever the status quo was at the time.

"We had paid a price for the privileges we enjoyed—our homes, our cars, and household appliances," Smith wrote in his 2009 autobiography, *A Memoir of Grace*. "Many remembered the hardships

she stopped at an intersection in Orange County. Kay noticed a pretty young girl on the sidewalk waiting for a streetlight to change. It was obvious to Kay this young woman was high on drugs—so high, in fact, that she didn't know where she was or what she was doing. As the girl attempted to cross the street, Kay became anxious. Her heart went out to this young woman, knowing she was someone's daughter and her parents were probably worried.

"You know, they are desperately in need of Jesus," Kay told her husband shortly after her experience.

"We've got to reach them. They have to know a different way of life. They've got to know Jesus." When viewed through that prism, Chuck chose to get on board. Besides, baptism might mean these odd-looking kids could finally get a decent bath.

Kay practically forced Chuck to drive to nearby beaches in Orange County, considered the weed and LSD mecca at the time. There was a reason for that: The Haight-Ashbury "Summer of Love" scene was quickly turning into something else.

"I went through Haight-Ashbury in its glory, all of these psychedelic buildings . . . it was a real culture there," recalled musician Chuck Girard. "And I went back a few years later and it was all drug dealers and all down-and-outers and free clinics because everybody had a disease. Everything seemed to come

THIS UTOPIA THEY TRIED TO CREATE WAS NOTHING MORE THAN A HELL ON EARTH.

crashing down . . . we were sitting there bewildered and thinking, *Where do we go from here?* That's when we started hearing about California."

More specifically, folks were washing up on the shores of Southern California, where Chuck and Kay Smith saw them during their weekend drives. While Chuck could only shake his head in contempt, Kay wept at the hundreds of lost souls and disillusioned young people who had uprooted themselves from fine middle-class homes for a lifestyle that promised peace, love, higher consciousness . . . and fairies and unicorns that failed to deliver.

All Kay saw were hippies, beach bums, and druggies, panhandling, dumpster diving, and roaming the streets while zonked out on pot or hallucinogens. These ragamuffins took shelter in pup tents, cardboard boxes, or smoke-filled VW vans camped out in beach parking lots, spending their days and nights wasting away their youth. Truly, this could have been an episode of *The Walking Dead*, but instead of flesh, the kids were eating psychedelic mushrooms, pot brownies, and lentils. She was determined to understand what motivated them (or, in this case, didn't) and declared to Chuck while cruising Main Street in Huntington Beach: "We have to meet a hippie!"

God answered that request fairly quickly when their daughter Janette started dating a young man named John Higgins at Southern California Christian College (now Vanguard University). Higgins had a taste of the Haight-Ashbury scene

CHUCK SMITH AND LONNIE FRISBEE WERE THE SPIRITUAL EQUIVALENT OF THE ODD COUPLE, BUT TOGETHER THEY WERE DYNAMITE . . . FOR A TIME.

LONNIE FRISBEE INTRODUCED MANY WEST COAST HIPPIES TO THE CHRISTIAN LIFE.

in San Francisco but quickly realized it was a vapid social experiment. In spite of the promises, he didn't witness much peace and love. Instead, he saw plenty of violence, sexual assault, manipulation, deceit, and heavy drug use. The utopia they tried to create was nothing more than a hell on earth, so Higgins returned to college for his education and began turning to God for his answers.

Higgins often spread the good news of salvation to hitchhikers, sharing the gospel with them whenever he could. One of those hitchhikers was a twenty-year-old who bore more than a passing resemblance to Jesus with his long brown hair and a bushy mustache and beard. His name was Lonnie Frisbee. And like Higgins, Frisbee had dropped out of college and dived headlong into the hippie movement, ingesting hallucinogenic drugs, practicing hypnotism, and even experimenting in occultic and mystical practices.

Sometime in 1967, Frisbee received a vision from the Lord revealing that he was going to use

him as "a light to thousands of other people." He was absolutely fervent in his witness to others about Christ, becoming involved in a ministry called "The Living Room," situated in the middle of the Haight-Ashbury district, and delivering hot gospel to the counterculture youth of the City by the Bay. One of the people he tried to reach was a recent parolee named Charles Manson, who told everyone he was Jesus and the devil while gulping down bowls of homemade soup.

"He would put us down for what we were doing in the community," Frisbee said. "Of course, this was while he was enjoying our delicious soup! So, anyway, Manson would come into our mission, eat our food, and mock us."

23

CALVARY CHAPEL HELD MONTHLY BAPTISMS AT PIRATE'S COVE IN NEWPORT BEACH, CALIFORNIA. HUNDREDS ATTENDED THESE BAPTISMS, WHICH STARTED THEIR CHRISTIAN WALKS.

Frisbee also drifted back and forth between San Francisco and Orange County, hitchhiking and telling others what Christ had done for him.

When Higgins was asked to deliver a hippie to the Smiths for enlightenment, he went big. He showed up with Frisbee on their doorstep in 1968. Frisbee sported a white, loose linen shirt, bell-bottom jeans with tinkling bells sewn in the hem of his cuffs, and a confident smile on his sun-kissed face. Higgins rang the doorbell, and the Smiths appeared together. Chuck's first thought was probably that while he might never get Frisbee off his couch, at least the soap in his shower wouldn't disappear.

According to Greg Laurie, this was a historical moment, even if it looked like the beginning of an intergenerational war.

"It was like when John Lennon met Paul McCartney or Steve Jobs met Steve Wozniak. Or when nitro met glycerin," said Laurie, who was not only part of this new phenomenon but also over the years became Chuck Smith's most successful and enduring protégé, preaching and evangelizing to millions. "Lonnie Frisbee and Chuck Smith were the same ontological species; aside from that, they had nothing in common in terms of personality, life experience, background, or appearance. But they both knew Jesus, and when Lonnie crossed Chuck and Kay's threshold, something big and volatile was about to happen that only God could orchestrate."

As Higgins and Frisbee settled themselves into the Smiths' antiseptic living room, Frisbee gave them the lowdown on hippiedom and the counterculture. He told them how this new classification of humanity thought, what motivated them, and what they were rebelling against. The Smiths hung on his every word, even finding him strangely engaging and warm. They were especially impressed by Frisbee's personal relationship with Jesus. Smith later recalled the way Frisbee talked about faith, saying it was as if he had just come from a meeting with Jesus himself. Their fascination turned to compassion. The Smiths invited Frisbee to stay with them a few weeks in an attempt to learn more. Frisbee informed his kind hosts that he had just married a dewy bride—a young Christian lass, formerly of the drug scene—and he wanted to thumb his way back to San Francisco, fetch her, and

AND GOD WAS CLEARLY AT WORK.

bring her to stay with them too. Would the Smiths mind? No, astonishingly, the Smiths would not mind. Seismic change was occurring in the Smith household. Their friends couldn't help but notice.

Frisbee's influence was soon felt at the church. Droves of barefooted and Jesus-sandaled hippies, reeking of patchouli and sporting beads, feathers, tie-dye shirts, embroidered jeans, tunics, head-bands, bell-bottoms, granny glasses, Wyatt Earp mustaches, and traditional Indian saris began fil-ing into Smith's Wednesday night services, raising the eyebrows and taking the breath away from his older, conservative congregation. Some of these interlopers sat cross-legged in the aisles, sporting Native American headgear (imagine how well that might go over today!), while others occupied the entire front row. Some even poked their toes through the communion cup holders on the backs of the pews. They were not a shy bunch, and they didn't play around with religion either. They were serious about their Christian faith and hungered for God's word. Those Wednesday nights became a spiritual sanctuary for these "Jesus freaks."

"Their hearts were so filled with the love of Jesus Christ, and everybody just immediately fell in love with them, and it really wasn't a hard thing to accept them," Smith recalled to journalist Dan Wooding. "We had been teaching the people 1 John and that the real proof of the Christian life is loving. So, the people did love them and embrace them, and so it was an exciting experience."

Actually, it was a once-in-a-lifetime expe-rience. And God clearly was at work.

There was no fire and brimstone, no finger-pointing, no heavy guilt trips at these services. Calvary Chapel preached forgiveness through the blood of Christ. One of the regulars was musician Chuck Girard, who had experienced success in his teens with a couple of Top 20 hits. Girard hung out with Brian Wilson and dabbled in LSD, hashish, marijuana, and Eastern philosophies. But he was a

CALVARY CHAPEL GREW LIKE WILDFIRE AS HIPPIES FLOODED THE SERVICES. IT EXPANDED SO QUICKLY THAT THEY HAD TO MOVE OVERFLOW CROWDS INTO A 1,600-SEAT TENT. LATER, THEY BUILT A NEW SANCTUARY.

THEY WERE TRUE BELIEVERS, NOT SUNDAY CHRISTIANS.

hippie on a quest and found tranquility in this particular house of worship.

"I walked inside and was overwhelmed by the sense of power I felt," Girard later said. "I had taken more than five hundred LSD trips and had some powerful experiences under the influence of drugs, but never had I felt a power like that night at Calvary Chapel."

The same overpowering feeling enveloped Girard's friend and bandmate Tommy Coomes, who put it this way: "Within a few weeks we had all went to Calvary Chapel and we all got radically saved, and that spun the whole thing around. So for me after that there was no turning back. This wasn't just a good idea. This was darkness to light and loneliness to joy."

Soon space became a real issue. The explosive growth forced Smith to build a new church to accommodate the newcomers who now numbered around three hundred people. When more came, they filled up all the pews *and* any available spot on the floor. They went to double services, then triple. The church then doubled the size of its auditorium and expanded to the outside patio, where the overflow listened to what was going on inside. The crowds grew so big that the county sent a fire

marshal to keep the youths from blocking the aisle. The marshal himself ended up getting saved during the altar call at the conclusion of the service.

Calvary erected a 1,600-seat tent and held three Sunday morning services in addition to Bible studies or concerts on most nights to handle the overflow. When that wasn't enough, they built a new sanctuary in Costa Mesa, but not before redesigning it three times to address the hordes and streams of young people who kept coming for services. These hippies multiplied like bunnies, only hairier and not as cuddly.

The Smiths also began inviting and allowing people to stay in their home, which today doesn't sound like a very sane idea. Permanent wet rings on the coffee table were the least of their worries. At one point, Chuck and Kay shoehorned thirty-five people into their two-bedroom abode, building bunks in the garage. Kids crashed on every available spot on the floor. One even slept in their bathtub. They also baptized their houseguests in their small backyard swimming pool.

In May 1968, the Smiths rented a second home in Costa Mesa, California, as a Christian communal crash pad for hippies to be known as "The House of Miracles." When they outgrew that space, a real estate

LOVE SONG APPEARING FOR
THEIR DESERT PROMO.

agent they knew offered a nine-unit motel (the Blue Top, formerly a house of prostitution during World War II) in Newport Beach that he owned for use as another Christian commune. About a half dozen more of these communal homes sprouted up over the course of the next year. The growth was God-ordained, yes . . . however, it was still insanity.

But it wasn't a scam for a free bowl of stew, a cup of coffee, and a place to crash. The kids obeyed the rules of the church. They weren't out in the parking lot secretly blowing bowls of hash. And they were diligent in their faith, evangelizing to others while still babes in Christ. They were true believers, not Sunday Christians. But their Sunday best didn't include shoes or ties. They looked the way they looked, and they practiced their faith their way. As for the music they heard at services, the style they were subjected to just wasn't their thing. They wanted something else, but *something else* didn't exist.

Yet.

Chuck Girard and a group of his friends first attended after a hitchhiker told them about what was happening at Calvary. They showed up, got saved, and then were baptized. They began attending regularly, which didn't go unnoticed by Frisbee. In February 1970, they struck up a casual conversation, and when Frisbee discovered they were musicians and writing songs for the Lord, he asked when he could hear them play. One of them piped up, "We have our guitars in the van. Why not right now?"

They sang their heartfelt songs for Frisbee, who was overcome with emotion. He sensed an alliance between their music and his preaching. Their songs would be a perfect fit for his Saturday night service. The next day Girard, Jay Traux, and Tommy Coomes visited Chuck Smith and told him they had been saved at Calvary a few weeks before. They asked if they could play a few songs at the service.

They told Smith that the Lord had given them a song. He nodded but remained poker-faced. They played "Welcome Back," a simple but touching song about returning to Jesus.

"I was fearful; but when I heard it, I broke down crying," Smith said. He asked them to play it at the Saturday service, but they mentioned they might have a small problem, man. One of their bandmates, Fred Fields, was in the Orange County jail for marijuana possession and wasn't getting out until that evening. Even if Fields got out that day, he had to be processed before going home and cleaning up. Through the grace of God and a bail bondsman, Fields did make it to Frisbee's service that evening, and the place exploded.

The group, known as Love Song, became the first mainstream Christian rock band and was considered "The Beatles of Jesus Rock."

And that moment was christened the birth of modern-day worship and praise music. Eventually, mainstream church slowly changed, and to the surprise of even the most stoic churchgoers, guitars, drums, and all types of modern instruments became acceptable for the first time in the church. Of course, such music is prevalent in sanctuaries all across the nation today.

Acoustic guitars and tambourines had started this evolution in the narthex. Now they were poised to "come forward" to the platform and then be launched out of the church and into halls, marquees, clubs, and arenas. Contemporary Christian music was about to be born.

THAT MOMENT WAS CHRISTENED THE BIRTH OF MODERN-DAY WORSHIP AND PRAISE MUSIC.

CHAPTER 3

JESUS ROCK(S)

There's a classic spot in Newport Beach, California called Pirate's Cove. It lies at the foot of short bluffs, leading out to a narrow promontory. On Sunday mornings throughout the early 1970s, along with the usual sunbathers, surfers, and dog walkers, as many as five hundred young people gathered to be baptized in the waves. For the congregation of Calvary Chapel, these baptisms

Outside of Orange County, no one knew a small but powerful revolution was taking hold in the church. Traditional hymns played on a Hammond and gospel choruses plunked out on a spinet were in the process of being replaced by new sounds of worship produced on acoustic guitars, drums, and tambourines.

After the night Love Song debuted their tie-dyed sound, there was a hunger for more "Jesus

JESUS ROCK(S)

became a monthly outing. Like everything else going on at the church, it was an unconventional approach to Christianity. No baptismal font, no stained glass windows, no choir. Just Chuck Smith, Lonnie Frisbee, a handful of other Calvary Chapel pastors, hundreds of hippies, and a sea of fresh salt water. It looked like something you might have seen on the shores of the Sea of Galilee more than two thousand years ago. It wasn't only hippies though. People of all ages were impacted by this youth revival.

Music," which is what they were beginning to call it.

Outside of Costa Mesa, no one knew about it. The music certainly wasn't played on the radio, record labels didn't dare produce it for mass consumption, and it wasn't being featured at any concert venue. But a year later it would be on the cover of *TIME* magazine.

That issue—June 21, 1971—heralded the change. It sported a pop art psychedelic Jesus gazing serenely from clouds and proclaimed "The Jesus Revolution."

Inside, a reporter captured the phenomenon of the countercultural embrace of the Son of God through a series of vignettes, including the unlikely pairing of a chrome-domed, middle-aged preacher and a semi-employed street proselytizer with an Old Testament beard but a new rap.

"It is a startling development for a generation that has been constantly accused of tripping out or copping out with sex, drugs and violence," the

magazines and national television news reports alongside images of the two baptizing hundreds at a time in the Pacific Ocean.

Greg Laurie was a firsthand witness to the history unfolding. "When I first attended Calvary Chapel, the place was filled wall to wall with people sitting in the pews and on the floor covered in shag green carpeting," Laurie said. "We swayed in unison to the melody of songs like 'Thy Loving Kindness'

article stated. "Now, embracing the most persistent symbol of purity, selflessness and brotherly love in the history of Western man, they are afire with a Pentecostal passion for sharing their new vision with others. Fresh-faced, wide-eyed young girls and earnest young men badger businessmen and shoppers on Hollywood Boulevard, near the Lincoln Memorial, in Dallas, in Detroit and in Wichita, 'witnessing' for Christ with breathless exhortations."

Following the *TIME* magazine story, Chuck Smith and Lonnie Frisbee were featured in several

and 'We Are One in the Spirit.' The place was simply filled with God's Holy Spirit. I did not realize it at the time, but I had walked smack-dab into the middle of a spiritual awakening."

The network of House of Miracles communes, crash pads, and coffeehouses also began doing outreach concerts with Smith or Frisbee preaching, with the latter calling forth the Holy Spirit and the newly formed bands playing the music.

Something was stirring. The Jesus Revolution was leaking from coffeehouses, communes, and

"I HAD WALKED SMACK-DAB INTO THE MIDDLE OF A SPIRITUAL AWAKENING."

high school and college campuses and into the popular consciousness.

Calvary Chapel not only brought new Christians from the waves but also ushered in new bands. At least a dozen acts sprouted from the church following Love Song. These bands performed almost nightly at Calvary Chapel, which they did for free because it was an expression of their creativity, an extension of their faith, and their own form of ministry. But faith doesn't always finance instruments, strings, amps, wheels, or gas

money, and it doesn't always put food (in this case, lentils and brown rice) on the table.

"How were we going to tell our generation about Jesus? We knew we had to make a record and knew we had to find our own way," said Love Song's Tommy Coomes. "There was just no Contemporary Christian music industry at all."

Chuck Smith saw a way to make that happen.

In 1971, he formed Maranatha! Music, a non-profit Christian music record label to make what was heard in the church more widely available and provide an outlet for the musical talent that emerged from Calvary Chapel. *Maranatha* is the Aramaic word for "Come, oh Lord." The songs and albums created through this label became the vanguard of Jesus Music and the worship music genre of that time.

And with every yin there's a yang. Yang in this case was Andraé Crouch, a black gospel singer, songwriter, arranger, record producer, and pastor based out of Los Angeles. Crouch initially made a name for himself in gospel circles with his group Andraé Crouch and the Disciples but was embraced by the Jesus Movement. His music found a sweet spot with listeners in *Take the Message Everywhere*, released in 1968 by Light Records, a Waco, Texas–based gospel music publisher. Crouch's mixture of feel-good gospel, soul, and funk transcended the divide between church and mainstream music, earning him the title of "Father of Modern Gospel." But the neatest hat trick was that Crouch's music broke down race barriers between blacks and

CHUCK SMITH PROUDLY HOLDING A COPY OF MARANATHA! MUSIC'S FIRST OFFICIAL RELEASE, *THE EVERLASTIN' LIVING JESUS MUSIC CONCERT* (1971).

34

whites, not unlike Motown concerts. His audiences were usually mixed in a time when the two races barely fraternized. He found new life as a crossover artist with young Christians, connecting with them through their faith and love of music. And for many black and white youths, he was their first introduction to gospel music.

"Andraé was probably one of the very best bridges," said Grammy Award-winning music icon and songwriter Bill Gaither. "Many of his concerts is what heaven should be like."

The very first concert five-time Grammy artist Steven Curtis Chapman saw was Andraé Crouch and the Disciples, and it rocked his world.

He recalled in 2020: "When I sat in the room and experienced what could happen when you take the passion of gospel music with great players and great singers and great musicians and the truth of God's word and God's grace and music, and then perform

that live, I mean I was hooked immediately when I first heard it. I was like, 'I WANNA DO THAT!'"

So what was Crouch's secret sauce?

"When we like songs in gospel and it hits that part of the soul or the mind that brings back familiarity to the person or to the listeners, I think we zero in on something that will always be needed," Crouch told *NPR* in 2015.

Record labels like Light Records usually depend on a flagship artist like Andraé Crouch to launch their product. Chuck Smith didn't have any marquee names to push out to the world, but

FOR HIM WHO HAS EARS TO HEAR BY KEITH GREEN (1977, SPARROW RECORDS). THE DEBUT RELEASE BY THE PIANIST AND SINGER.

BILLY GRAHAM DELIVERING THE KEYNOTE ADDRESS IN DALLAS' COTTON BOWL FOR EXPLO '72, A SEMINAL MOMENT FOR CONTEMPORARY CHRISTIAN MUSIC.

he had more than fifteen artists/acts in his stable. They included homespun Christian names like Sweet Comfort Band, Parable, Mustard Seed Faith, Children of the Day, Blessed Hope, and of course, Love Song. The label also nurtured other talented artists like Debby Kerner, a pioneering children's musician, and The Way, a Christian band reminiscent of the pop-rock group America. While not as well-known as Love Song, The Way had a string of hits over the years and a dedicated following. One of the artists that Maranatha! did not record but who was in the Calvary Chapel scene was Keith Green, who reached legendary status a few years later as a Contemporary Christian music artist.

Maranatha! Music's first official issue was called *The Everlastin' Living Jesus Music Concert* (1971). Ironically, it wasn't actually a live concert album but a sampler of various artists performing the best music coming out of Calvary Chapel. It sold more than two hundred thousand units, making a tidy return on the investment from the initial $4,000 it took to produce. It remains one of the most important releases in Contemporary Christian music history. Today, the album is viewed as the dawn of Jesus Music.

One of those used copies wended its way across the country to Kenova, West Virginia, where a teenager named Michael W. Smith first became acquainted with the album.

"I remember I walked into a thrift store and went over to this record bin," recalled the Grammy

"I BELIEVE THIS IS A GREAT AND HISTORIC GATHERING."

artist who has sold an estimated twenty million albums throughout his career. "In this record bin there was this big red Maranatha! sign on this white cover and it was called *The Everlastin' Living Jesus Music Concert*. I picked it up and turned it around, and it was all these people with long hair, and I could tell all of these songs were about Jesus. I remember thinking, *That's what I want to do!* I bought that record, and it changed my life."

The print runs on most of the albums were low (usually ten thousand or less) and made on shoestring budgets. One group, Children of the Day, a Christian version of the Mamas & the Papas, actually hit up Chuck Smith for a $900 loan to record their debut album, *Come to the Waters*. Smith kindly floated them the cash. Predictably, many of these recordings were primitive sounding and, according to John Styll, "the stuff, honestly, wasn't very good... but it was the beginning of something."

Maranatha! used a striking red downward dove as its logo, which was a symbol of the Holy Spirit. It was more than appropriate as these artists and musicians were led by the Holy Spirit in their quest to spread hope through their music. And they needed all the help they could get because Maranatha! Music had very limited distribution save for church gift shops, Christian bookstores, and mail orders. (Remember that?!)

"We literally put those albums in a Sunday school room and priced them at $4.98, and people would buy them," said Love Song's Tommy Coomes. "They would buy five of them and give them to all their friends."

Everything was poised for a breakout from Southern California except a national audience. That finally came in June 1972.

Explo '72 (short for "Spiritual Explosion") was a high-water mark for the Jesus Movement that attempted to make Christianity relevant to the post-Aquarius generation. This paradigmatic event in the history of American evangelicalism introduced a new music phenomenon to a large audience.

Hosted by Campus Crusade for Christ (now called Cru), an interdenominational organization committed to evangelism and discipleship for college and high school students, Explo '72 congregated eighty thousand young people from seventy-five countries to praise Jesus. Dallas, Texas, played host to the massive four-day event, which included

EXPLO '72 INCLUDED EVANGELISM CLASSES, GUEST SPEAKERS, AND PACKED CONCERTS THROUGHOUT DALLAS, DRAWING AN ESTIMATED 200,000 PEOPLE.

evangelism classes, seminars, and esteemed guest speakers, concluding with packed concerts at venues spread throughout Dallas, including the Cotton Bowl. An estimated two hundred thousand people attended the music events. Billy Graham, cosponsor of Explo and the keynote speaker, referred to it as the "Christian Woodstock."

"I wanted to come and identify with [the youth] because I believe this is a great and historic gathering," Billy told a television news reporter who asked why he came to the Lone Star state. "This is going to be a moment in the history of Dallas and a moment in the history of the world." At the conclusion of the event, Graham called Explo '72 one of the greatest experiences of his life.

LIFE magazine, a preeminent weekly publication that chronicled the twentieth century through exceptional photography and writing, dedicated a cover story to the spiritual gathering.

Johnny Cash hosted a star-studded and eclectic lineup that included Kris Kristofferson & Rita Coolidge, Larry Norman, Love Song, Andraé Crouch and the Disciples, Children of the Day, Randy Matthews, The Archers, and Phil Keaggy, the genre's first and most beloved guitar hero.

The timing was especially fortuitous for Love Song, whose self-titled debut album released the week before the big gig. As a result, *Love Song* sold approximately two hundred thousand units, and the group later received an offer from Ahmet Ertegun, cofounder and president of Atlantic Records, to switch over to his label. The band refused because they were fine where they were, ministering to saved and unsaved souls through their music.

"For me, the key thing was that Billy Graham got up and spoke," said Love Song's Chuck Girard. "There's all these people gathered together in the Cotton Bowl at night and hippies come out and we play. Rock 'n' roll is a music of rebellion, and so parents are like, 'Uh, this is so bad.' Billy gets up, speaks, and all of a sudden he opened their minds to the idea that this music that's born out of rebellion . . . maybe this could be appropriated to something that the Holy Spirit can use. It was sort of an affirmation. It was a seal of approval."

"MAYBE THIS COULD BE APPROPRIATED TO SOMETHING THAT THE HOLY SPIRIT CAN USE."

The long-term impact of Explo '72 cannot be overstated. It brought an entire generation from around the world to Christianity by speaking to them on their ground, forever changing the lives of many who marched forward in their lives with Jesus as their Savior. The most obvious and lasting impact was the influence of Jesus Music, which just a few years later would be more commonly referred to as "Contemporary Christian music." The music itself inspired many people who would become the genre's mega acts in the 1970s and beyond. Explo '72 wasn't a pebble thrown in a pond. It was a boulder. And it produced big waves.

While audience members were mostly high school and college kids, a half-dozen record executives on hand saw a new and untapped market and lots of green. Word Record executive Billy Ray Hearn was present at Explo '72 and acted quickly, even though his label initially treated this emerging new market as a strange fad. Hearn started and ran Myrrh Records in 1972 and left for California, where he formed Sparrow Records in 1976. He proved to be one of the most prolific and influential Contemporary Christian music executives of all time, helping to shape the business into what it is today. His son Bill Hearn was equally influential in the Christian music industry and, in a way, remains a keeper of the flame.

Word was originally founded in 1951 by the Baylor University sports play-by-play guy, Jarrell F. McCracken, along with his friends, Henry SoRelle and Ted Snider. It started off with hymn and "sacred music" albums by the likes of George Beverly Shea and Frank Boggs in the 1950s and wisely expanded into other genres over the next few decades. That included inking several distribution deals with a Who's Who of Christian artists and subsidiary labels (Canaan, Myrrh, Dayspring, Light, Rejoice, Reunion, Star Song, and Solid Rock Records) that carried Southern gospel, Christian rock, pop, country, alternative, and praise and worship, and helped introduce Christian artists such as Amy Grant, Michael W. Smith, Sandi Patty, and Petra to mainstream audiences.

They also expanded their empire in 1960, opening a print publishing arm called Word Books, which released an overnight international best seller in 1965, *The Taste of New Wine*. This book, penned by Episcopal layman and first-time author Keith Miller, deeply impacted traditional evangelical thought through the fresh experience of a mainline believer.

THE TRANSFORMATION IN THE MUSIC SCENE WAS DRAMATIC . . .

SOMETHING HISTORIC IS GOING TO HAPPEN HERE.

EXPLO '72 IN DALLAS JUNE 12-17

A BUS ADVERTISEMENT FROM EXPLO '72
PROVED TO BE PROPHETIC IN PREDICTING
THE MAGNITUDE OF THE EVENT.

Word was not only becoming a premier Christian record label; it would also become an authoritative and influential voice in Christian communication for the next seventy years.

The transformation in the music scene was dramatic . . . a lot to pack into four years. In the time it takes to earn a college degree, a new generation had been brought into the church, a new type of music (and a new type of worship) had been created, and all of it had made its way from a small Southern California beach to the center of the nation's attention in the pages of *TIME*, *Rolling Stone*, *LIFE*, and *LOOK*. It was all happening so fast and few people knew what to make of it.

Or from it. In America, that means money. Ahmet Ertegun and Billy Ray Hearn were smart enough to see something no one else did. But other people were beginning to get the idea.

All of it was about to explode . . . and make a lot of cash registers ring.

CHAPTER 4

DAVID MEETS GOLIATH

In 1972, rock 'n' roll was king. It was undoubtedly the most popular form of entertainment in America at the time. More people went to concerts than to sporting events. Record sales also outpaced movie tickets. Rock stars weren't merely celebrities; they were gods who existed in their own pantheon.

Acts like the Rolling Stones, Led Zeppelin, the Who, Alice Cooper, and Three Dog Night

personalized jet on one of their album covers, *Rock and Roll Outlaws*.

They drank champagne from silver buckets. They proudly squeezed into their shiny leather pants, and almost all of them had shoulder-length hair, perhaps none as iconic as Robert Plant's curly golden locks. They lived in multimillion-dollar mansions and castles, built guitar-shaped swimming pools in their backyards, kept lions and

DAVID MEETS GOLIATH

played in front of tens of thousands of people in arenas and large outdoor stadiums. Tickets would set you back between five and ten dollars (that's roughly between thirty and sixty-five dollars in today's currency), if you could withstand festival seating and not going to the bathroom for several hours.

These rock gods no longer traveled in old vans or beat-up station wagons to their gigs. They sported limos and chartered planes as evidenced by Foghat's less-than-subtle inclusion of a

cheetahs as house pets, dated beautiful women way out of their league, and trashed luxury hotel rooms—required stops on the trip to glory. It was *Spinal Tap* on steroids.

Making Hollywood look like it had reverted back to the days of vaudeville and sawdust, the record industry had surpassed the $8 billion mark, eclipsing film revenue in a year that saw movie releases such as *The Godfather*, *Cabaret*, *Deliverance*, and *The Poseidon Adventure*, which crushed at the box office. Christian record executives wanted to mine some of that secular gold too.

Helping to bridge that gap were mainstream acts beginning to dip their toes into the Christian pool. Johnny Cash released *The Gospel Road*, a daring double LP from a feature film on Jesus that was his on-the-record testament of faith; Aretha Franklin's *Amazing Grace* ascended to No. 7 on *Billboard*'s album charts and went double-platinum.

in the popular culture, you can always find an entertainment executive with dollar signs in his eyes and a willingness to throw anything against the wall to stick. Even the Vatican sells papal bottle openers to visitors.

Jesus Rock had taken its baby steps and was now ready to stride. Love Song's sensational self-titled debut album didn't sell modestly like most other Maranatha! Music releases. The fact that it

It also garnered her a Grammy Award for Best Soul Gospel Performance; the Doobie Brothers' cover of the Byrds' "Jesus Is Just Alright" gave the band their second Top 40 single; Glen Campbell crossed over and scored on the country charts with "I Knew Jesus (Before He Was a Star)" while Helen Reddy's "I Don't Know How to Love Him" reached No. 13 on *Billboard*'s singles chart.

Films such as *Godspell*, *The Gospel Road*, and *Jesus Christ Superstar* were also trying to catch this wave of Jesus mania. When God goes mainstream

sold in the hundreds of thousands indicated serious potential. Christian record executives wisely put their chips on the table and won big.

David was about to become Goliath.

New Christian stars like Larry Norman, Love Song, Andraé Crouch, and Evie Tornquist began to emerge, and established veterans like Barry McGuire, Dion DiMucci, Bruce Cockburn, and Grammy artist B.J. Thomas ("Raindrops Keep Fallin' on My Head") were shedding their musical roots and embracing Jesus.

GRAMMY AWARD-WINNING ARTIST B.J. THOMAS AND PRODUCER CHRIS CHRISTIAN REVIEWING LYRICS AND MUSICAL CHARTS INSIDE NASHVILLE'S GOLDMINE STUDIO FOR THE *HOME WHERE I BELONG* SESSIONS.

Many of the early pop stars, especially those from the South like Thomas, grew up singing in the choirs of old-fashioned, down-home churches and felt moved to express their faith based on the music of their upbringing once they acquired pop success. For some reason, the influence of the simplicity and soul-rhythm style of gospel songs made for an easy transition into rock 'n' roll for these artists.

Thomas scored big with *Home Where I Belong*, an album produced by Chris Christian on Myrrh Records. It was the first Christian album certified gold (a half-million copies) and rejuvenated Thomas' career by turning him into the biggest contemporary Christian artist of his time. It also marked a big turning point for Christian music.

The acts themselves weren't the only ones shifting. Big-name producers such as Chris Christian, Phil Johnson, Brown Bannister, and Michael Omartian began to have their own ideas about the sound and direction of the music. Singer Pat Boone, who seemingly had his hand

in almost every type of business venture (he was once a majority owner of an American Basketball Association team called the Oakland Oaks but sold them after two seasons), even founded his own Jesus Music label, Lamb & Lion Records. It was distributed by MGM on the secular side and by the Word Records sales force in Christian bookstores. The label released his records and that of his daughter, Debby Boone, but also DeGarmo & Key, Dan Peek, Steve Green, Gary Chapman, and Dogwood, a folk/pop band who released the first pop Christian album in the Southern United States.

Chris Christian was already established as a singer-songwriter when he came to Nashville in early 1974. He was writing and recording advertising jingles for his new business, the Home Sweet Home Jingle Company. His steady job—the one that put food on the table—was as Opryland leader of the folk show band. He even used his clout to hire his friend, Brown Bannister, to play the fiddle. Problem was, Bannister didn't know how to play the fiddle, but he was convinced he could learn. And learn he did after five shows a day, six days a week.

Those things paid the bills, but Christian's true desire was to cut pop records, preferably hits. It came in handy that Christian had a great head for business. In addition to his jingles company, he formed a publishing house and was getting ready to build his own music studio in a home he had just purchased for $25,000.

Christian picked up a new job title when he called his friend Pat Boone and told him about a group he had heard at the Koinonia Coffeehouse that sounded a lot like Crosby, Stills & Nash but with Christian lyrics. He asked Boone if he could produce Dogwood for Boone's new Lamb & Lion label. He said yes. Christian produced Dogwood's first album, *After the Flood, Before the Fire*, which was released in 1975. The budget was $5,000.

Boone liked the fact that Dogwood sounded commercial and envisioned that one day pop radio wouldn't be afraid to play Christian songs. He agreed to the request by twenty-two-year-old Christian, even though he had never produced an album before.

"Pat Boone took a tremendous leap of faith on me because he was betting on a guy who had never produced an album for a group who had never recorded for a genre that hadn't been established," Christian said in amazement, nearly forty-five years later. "How many people can say that? Pat really put his money where his faith was. He rarely gets

"PAT REALLY PUT HIS MONEY WHERE HIS FAITH WAS."

the credit he deserves for his role in pushing this industry along."

Word Records executive Stan Moser heard and liked *After the Flood, Before the Fire* and offered Christian the job of producing B.J. Thomas's *Home Where I Belong*. After that album went gold, Moser tendered Christian a deal in 1976 to produce five albums a year for the next five years—an almost unheard-of opportunity that netted him $250,000 a year.

"I just happened to be the right guy at the right time," Christian said. "The ironic part was I had all this money to do albums but no artists," Christian said.

That soon wouldn't be a problem.

Christian's Goldmine Studio, located in the basement of his Nashville home, captured some great music and signaled the end of Music Row's burlap-and-barnwood sound. Goldmine cut some of the biggest Christian songs of all time and rewarded the producer for his efforts. Christian snagged nine

Grammy Award nominations from albums he produced and won four. He earned seven nominations for Dove Awards as an artist, songwriter, and producer. He ended up winning five of the seven, including New Artist of the Year in 1976. Five years later he launched his own music label, Home Sweet Home Records, in Dallas, Texas. He still owns it.

Music was becoming more professionally produced with a crisper, slicker pop/rock sound. Some could also bring down the house. Chicago's Resurrection Band was considered Jesus Rock's answer to Led Zeppelin and are often credited as the forerunner to Christian metal in the 1980s.

The new Christian artists weren't amateurs who played in church basements; they now took advantage of first-rate facilities and professional engineers. When you heard an album by B.J. Thomas, Dogwood, Phil Keaggy, Dennis Agajanian, 2nd Chapter of Acts, John Michael Talbot, or The Imperials, it didn't sound like an unsophisticated Maranatha! Music album from the early years.

And then there was Keith Green.

Green was a prodigy from Brooklyn, New York, learning to play the ukulele by age three, the guitar at five, and the piano at seven. In addition, he was a singer-songwriter and transcendent artist who converted from Judaism to Christianity. By age twelve, Green had written several original songs and was signed to a five-year recording contract with Decca Records, home to Buddy Holly, the Rolling Stones, Van Morrison, the Who, and the Moody Blues. *TIME* magazine even wrote a short article on the pre-teenaged musical phenom.

Green strived to be more than a musician, however. After his conversion, he worked in prison outreach, helped in rehab centers, and supported several missions. Bob Dylan not only held him up as a musical peer but also as a spiritual mentor.

Green broke musical and marketing barriers, the latter pleasing fans and making record executives bite their nails in horror. *Relevant* magazine writer Jesse Carey noted: "He implemented a then-unheard-of 'whatever you can afford' pricing system for some of his music (even if it meant giving it away)—all the way back in 1979. And, long before TOMS [the shoe company], he embraced the 'buy-one, give-one' model, requesting that Christian bookstores that sold his album give another to the customer for he or she to give to a friend."

Green was a new star; Larry Norman was a big star—big enough to call his own shots and gather several emerging Christian artists together

GREEN BROKE MUSICAL AND MARKETING BARRIERS.

KEITH GREEN WAS UNCONVENTIONAL BY NATURE, WHETHER TAKING PEOPLE IN OFF THE STREET TO DISCIPLE THEM OR IN CHALLENGING HIS LABEL TO LET HIM GIVE HIS MUSIC TO THOSE WHO COULDN'T AFFORD IT.

on his new label, Solid Rock Records. Having so much invested in Norman, Word Records struck a distribution deal with Norman in 1975 that gave him total creative control of his music and others, so much so that he was able to legally appropriate all of their publishing—not under their noses, but right

in their faces. This was a monumental achievement and the first time ever that a Christian artist had made this type of deal.

By the end of the 1970s, some of rock's biggest icons were embracing Christianity—none bigger than John Lennon. The former Beatle was in his "househusband" stage at this point in his life, sitting out the latter half of the decade after having fulfilled his last record contract for Apple. So, he baked bread, changed diapers, and fed his son, Sean, during the day while his wife, Yoko Ono, ran their business affairs. With plenty of nannies to spell him, Lennon was free to explore yoga, mysticism, vegetarianism, and various forms of religion. (Near the end of his life, he referred to himself as a "Zen pagan.")

The man who once said the Beatles were more popular than Jesus came to Jesus himself in spring 1977 after watching Billy Graham preach at one of his televised Crusades. Bob Rosen, author of *Nowhere*

Man: The Final Days of John Lennon, is one of a handful of people who actually saw Lennon's private, handwritten diaries that he kept from 1975–1980. He recalled, "[Lennon] was watching Billy Graham sermons on TV because he found them entertaining. Then he had an epiphany. Apparently Graham's words got through to him and he accepted Jesus. It lasted about two weeks," Rosen said.

In that two-week period, the former Beatle considered himself a Christian and took his wife and their child to an Easter Sunday service. He was also prone to dropping "praise the Lord" and "thank you, Jesus" into odd spots in his conversations. He even wrote a song called "Amen," which was his musical version of "The Lord's Prayer." That didn't go over so well with his infamous wife.

Yoko Ono was not only a breaker of bands, but of faith. It was no secret she dabbled in "white magic," using numerology to do background checks on new and old friends, potential employees, and anyone she did business with. She also called on a cadre of tarot card readers to plot her every maneuver, including travel plans, business negotiations, and investments (including ancient Egyptian artifacts, which she believed held magical power).

She eventually lured Lennon away from God to the point where he used tarot cards for almost every decision. But like his time with the Maharishi in India, it was just a phase.

RANDY STONEHILL'S *WELCOME TO PARADISE* (1976) WAS RELEASED BY LARRY NORMAN'S SOLID ROCK RECORDS AND BECAME A CCM CLASSIC.

Lennon's contemporary, Bob Dylan, had a legitimate spiritual metamorphosis, which started in November 1978. That's when a fan tossed a tiny silver cross onstage in San Diego to the legendary singer-songwriter, who picked it up, placed it in his pocket, and forgot about it until the following night while in a Tucson, Arizona, hotel. Feeling a little melancholy and perhaps alone and isolated in his room, he fished the cross out of his pocket and placed it around his neck. It felt good. Really good.

The timing of this event coincided with the recent conversions of his girlfriend, Mary Alice Artes, and bandmates Steven Soles, David Mansfield, and T-Bone Burnett. Artes, an actress (*She Came to the Valley*), introduced Dylan to members of the Vineyard Christian Fellowship, which was cofounded in 1974 by pastors Ken Gulliksen and John Wimber after they split off from Calvary Chapel. Lonnie Frisbee also ended up there after he and Chuck Smith had a disagreement over demons. Frisbee believed in them, and Smith did not relish associating with the more fringe aspects

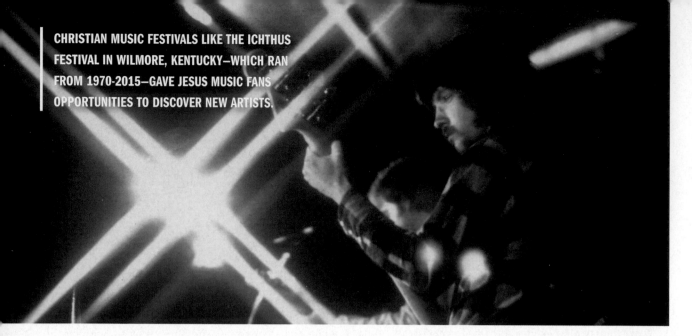

of Christianity, such as the Gadarene swine. Smith was a meat and potatoes Christian; Frisbee liked his Christianity far out.

But back to Dylan . . .

Through Artes's soft but firm prompting, Dylan eventually received Christ. He recalled it as "a knee-buckling experience."

"Jesus put his hand on me," Dylan told journalist Karen Hughes. "It was a physical thing. I felt it. I felt it all over me. I felt my whole body tremble. The glory of the Lord knocked me down and picked me up."

Dylan's conversion bled into his Christian trilogy of *Slow Train Coming*, *Saved*, and *Shot of Love*. His song "Gotta Serve Somebody" from 1979's *Slow Train Coming* even won a Grammy for Best Rock Vocal Performance by a Male. But that's where the accolades stopped. Dylan paid the price when, in his newfound exuberance, he put on an all-gospel show. Artistically, it was bold; commercially

speaking, it was a big mistake. Fans recoiled in horror when he played this new music instead of the hits, and Dylan was soundly booed at his own concerts. He was also widely mocked by the rock press and mainstream journalists. John Lennon even piled on by penning a profanity-laced parody of Dylan's song "Serve Somebody," which he called "Serve Yourself." In his diary tape from September 5, 1979, Lennon was recorded as saying: "'Gotta Serve Somebody' . . . guess he [Dylan] wants to be a waiter now." (Several

"THE GLORY OF THE LORD KNOCKED ME DOWN AND PICKED ME UP."

versions of the unreleased song can be heard on YouTube.com.) Today, Bob Dylan considers himself both a Christian and a Jew; a wise move considering his need to continue appealing to a wide variety of fans after his Christian phase.

Other high-profile artists from the music scene were getting burned out on sex, drugs, and rock 'n' roll. They included soul singer Al Green, Donna Summer, Arlo Guthrie, Alice Cooper, Bernie Leadon of the Eagles, Joe English of Wings, Bonnie Bramlett of Delaney & Bonnie, Philip Bailey of Earth, Wind & Fire, Mark Farner of Grand Funk Railroad, Richie Furay of Buffalo Springfield and Poco, Roger McGuinn of the Byrds, Dan Peek of America, Rick Wakeman of Yes, John Schlitt of Head East, Rick Cua of Outlaws, Reggie Vinson (who played and wrote songs for Alice Cooper), Graeham Goble of the Little River Band, and Randy Cutlip, a keyboardist for Three Dog Night, who after twenty years of heavy drug abuse, could barely walk when he left the band. Cutlip's conversion was as much a resurrection as anything else. Each of these artists had their taste of wine and weed . . . and decided God was a better high without the hangover.

Most of those performers could have gone to any record label and landed a solo deal. For Christian artists, it was another story. They sold fine in their own bubble, but they needed more exposure.

This came courtesy of two Christian radio stations, which emerged in the mid-1970s. The first one was KBHL (Kept By His Love) in Lincoln, Nebraska; the second was KYMS in Southern California. Though it was the second Contemporary Christian music station, it soon achieved preeminence.

These outlets opened the floodgates and proved that the genre would work in a station format. Through their ad sales, revenue, and eye-popping ratings, they discovered that Jesus was "just alright" with a lot of people.

A DJ PLAYING SOME OF THE NEWEST MUSIC AT KCLB, K-LOVE'S PREDECESSOR, IN NORTHERN CALIFORNIA.

CHAPTER 5

A MARRIAGE
MADE IN HEAVEN

t was post-Vietnam. Post–political assassination. Domestic terrorism was looking like a dot in the rearview mirror. President Nixon was gone, and Ford was headed for the door. People wanted something new. They wanted to have fun. And they wanted to dress up and look good. The unofficial hippie uniform—denims, khaki army jacket, and headband—was ditched in favor of a slick suit, gold chains, silk shirt, and

Meanwhile, down in Nashville, Tennessee, an aspiring fifteen-year-old singer-songwriter was quietly making waves. Amy Grant started out singing in church. At home she listened to mainstream music because that's what her parents and older sisters listened to: the Beatles, Elvis Presley, Aretha Franklin, the Jackson 5, Carole King, James Taylor, Elton John, Joni Mitchell, and Judy Collins. Her first concert was Sonny & Cher. She was probably the

A MARRIAGE MADE IN HEAVEN

platform shoes. For women, it was skin-tight designer jeans, sequined shirts, feathered hair, aqua blue eyeshadow, and high heels.

People just wanted to feel good and party. And party they did. The nation's bicentennial gave them a pretty good reason. It also gave them back their pride despite double-digit inflation, gasoline shortages, and the twin embarrassments of Watergate and Vietnam. And even though America was changing and advancing, a good number of God-fearing folks still lived by their own rules in the country's Bible Belt.

only woman there not ironing her hair or wearing a crop top or an Emilio Pucci dress, but they had her, babe.

That was the music she liked, and she wondered why there couldn't be something like that at church. She sensed there could be.

"When I realized, like everybody else when I was on my own faith journey, I kept thinking, *Is there some way . . . can't you sing something in addition to hymns that reflects life, the faith journey?*" Grant said.

She started out writing songs that students at her all-girl private school, Harpeth Hall, would listen to. Grant performed in front of her church youth group, for weddings, and on Saturday evenings at Koinonia, a bookstore across the street from Belmont Avenue Church of Christ. She was inspired to write her own songs in the bookstore's coffeehouse. As influential as Calvary Chapel Costa Mesa was to the Jesus Movement in California, Koinonia

also a talented audio engineer who worked for producer Chris Christian at the time. (Bannister later became a major producer in his own right, forming his own independent label, Vireo Records, in 1991. To date he has twenty-five Dove Awards and fourteen Grammys; has been named "Producer of the Year" five times by the Gospel Music Association; and is a member of the Gospel Music Hall of Fame.)

was equally so in Nashville and to Contemporary Christian music.

Instinctively, Grant knew her schoolmates might not go to church to listen to this kind of music, but they might listen to her songs and be inspired.

"I thought, *Man, music could sure bridge the gap*, because you can tell people about the love of God but you're not like pressing them for a response," Grant said. "You sort of float a song out there . . ."

Her voice floated and caught the ear of Brown Bannister, her youth minister. He was

Bannister offered Grant a once-in-a-lifetime opportunity.

"Look, Amy, I have free time at a recording studio," he said. She brought a friend along and cut the tunes fairly quickly. Bannister said he'd make a few cassette copies for her to give to friends and loved ones.

While Bannister was burning cassettes for Grant, Chris Christian walked in and heard the demos. Christian, who was still in the early stages of his production deal with Word Records, was on

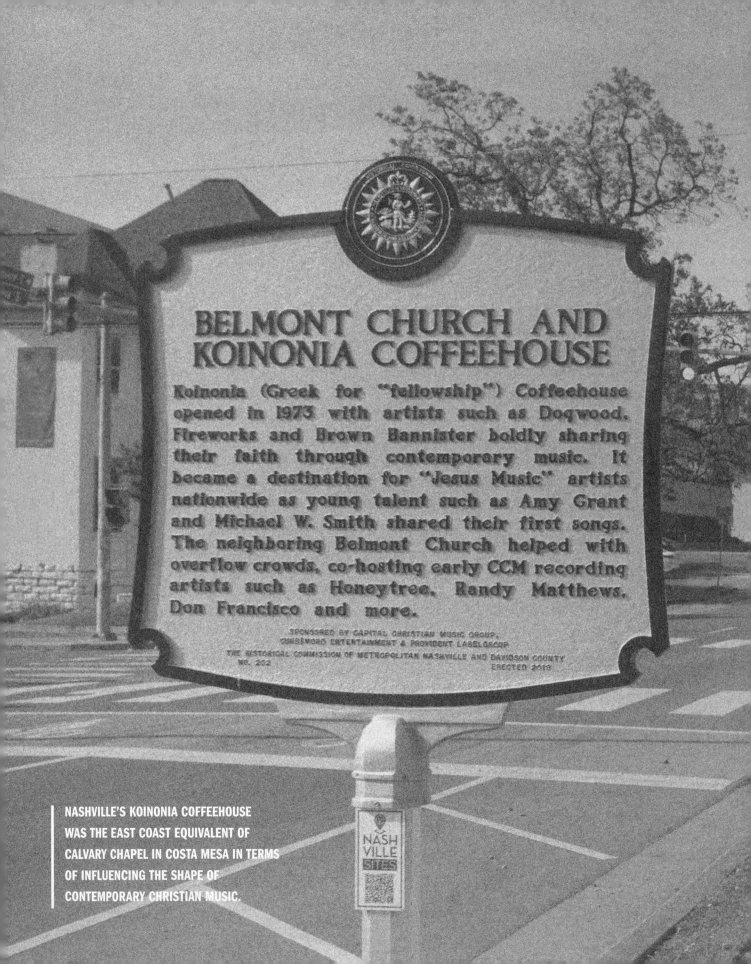

BELMONT CHURCH AND KOINONIA COFFEEHOUSE

Koinonia (Greek for "fellowship") Coffeehouse opened in 1973 with artists such as Dogwood, Fireworks and Brown Bannister boldly sharing their faith through contemporary music. It became a destination for "Jesus Music" artists nationwide as young talent such as Amy Grant and Michael W. Smith shared their first songs. The neighboring Belmont Church helped with overflow crowds, co-hosting early CCM recording artists such as Honeytree, Randy Matthews, Don Francisco and more.

SPONSORED BY CAPITAL CHRISTIAN MUSIC GROUP,
CURB/WORD ENTERTAINMENT & PROVIDENT LABELGROUP
THE HISTORICAL COMMISSION OF METROPOLITAN NASHVILLE AND DAVIDSON COUNTY
NO. 202
ERECTED 2019

NASHVILLE'S KOINONIA COFFEEHOUSE
WAS THE EAST COAST EQUIVALENT OF
CALVARY CHAPEL IN COSTA MESA IN TERMS
OF INFLUENCING THE SHAPE OF
CONTEMPORARY CHRISTIAN MUSIC.

the lookout for new artists and still hadn't signed anyone.

Bannister then played Christian a demo of her pop Christian songs. The producer knew Amy and her family—he had dated her older sister—so he listened intently.

He quickly concluded that Grant's songs were charismatic and genuine, but her voice and song-writing hadn't matured yet. She also didn't know how to breathe properly, but experience would be her best teacher.

"She's not that great of a singer, but she's sincere," Christian said. After all, she was only fifteen.

Regardless of Grant's shortcomings, Christian picked up the phone and called Stan Moser and told him that his production company, Home Sweet Home Productions, had signed its first artist.

This came as a great surprise to Grant, who wasn't seeking stardom or, for that matter, even a record deal. In fact, she thought a grand joke was being played on her when she learned Christian wanted to sign her and distribute her album through Word's subsidiary, Myrrh Records.

"It was a different time. An unobserved time," said Grant, who would continue her studies at Nashville's Vanderbilt University after graduating from high school. "We didn't have all the hoopla with social media. I went to high school and college and wrote songs and toured in the summertime, so it was a very nurturing, quiet way to start, unlike the high-pressure cooker that people find themselves in today."

"IT WAS A VERY NURTURING AND QUIET WAY TO START."

Grant cut her thirteen-song debut album, simply titled *Amy Grant*, in Christian's Gold Mine Studio, mostly after school and on weekends. The astute record producer noticed that Grant's alto voice was similar to Karen Carpenter's and wanted to duplicate her sound for a Christian audience. He even brought in The Carpenters' bassist, Joe Osborn, to help recreate their hallmark sound. He also recruited an A-list team of studio musicians, including Reggie Young, who played lead guitar on Elvis Presley's 1969 comeback album, *From Elvis in Memphis*, and was a member of Chips Moman's house band at Memphis's American Sound Studio.

Amy Grant was released in early February 1977 on Myrrh Records to little fanfare. However,

AMY GRANT WAS A TEENAGER WHEN SHE RELEASED *MY FATHER'S EYES* (MYRRH, 1979). THE TITLE TRACK BECAME HER FIRST CHRISTIAN NUMBER-ONE HIT.

it slowly evolved. When Christian heard "Beautiful Music," a song one of his staff writers named Lanier Ferguson wrote, he produced it like a pop single. It received a lot of airplay too. "Old Man's Rubble" and "What a Difference You've Made" also got love from the radio, and the record moved with slow and steady momentum. It sold incredibly well for a rookie artist—fifty thousand units in the first three months—and increasingly more in the run up to her second release, 1979's *My Father's Eyes*.

Contemporary Christian Music magazine publisher John Styll said Grant's first album wasn't stylistically or musically overwhelming, but it was "unexpectedly huge." That was due in large part to Grant's unhip, girl-next-door image.

"[Amy Grant] had kind of a bad cover," Styll said. "She didn't sing great. But people loved her, and they loved those songs."

Indeed, they did. Grant's first album received national radio airplay on gospel radio, but not on Contemporary Christian radio or in Nashville. That was in the future.

"PEOPLE LOVED HER AND THEY LOVED THOSE SONGS."

Surprisingly, Nashville did not have a pop Christian music station of its own. The first place to lay claim to that honor was KGER in Long Beach, California. Since 1974, one hour of Jesus Music was broadcast each week on KGER, a traditional religious station. The rest of the programming was back-to-back preaching like most religious stations. John Styll's "Hour of Praise" featured local Christian acts, many out of Calvary Chapel.

"It was both a vanguard show and an avant-garde show," Styll said. And at times, it was almost a no-show.

"Hour of Praise" was broadcast daily at 3:00 p.m. Styll recorded the show, typically after noon, on a ten-inch reel-to-reel tape in a Newport Beach studio. Once he finished, Styll grabbed the reel, cradled it in his arm like a football, and jumped in his Ford Mustang. He then barreled towards the KGER studios in Long Beach like Steve McQueen in *Bullitt*. At least, he tried to barrel like Steve McQueen. It was a thirty-mile jaunt through heavy traffic—Southern California traffic, "c'mon, c'mon, c'mon"—and Styll often arrived just in the nick of time with sweat trickling down his temples and his heart near bursting out of his chest. He regularly showed up inside the studio without a second to spare, just as the closing comments were being made on the prior show. A wily producer had an album of Christian music ready to play in case Styll arrived late, but he never did.

In March 1975, KBHL in Lincoln, Nebraska, and KYMS out of Orange County both hit the airwaves with great fanfare.

KBHL ("Kept By His Love") started its first broadcast by proclaiming, "We're on the air! Thank you, Lord!" Locals and businesses felt the same way. A local A&W drive-through sold hamburgers and root beer and enthusiastically pushed KBHL bumper stickers on its patrons, helping to get the word out and pump the station. It was also a marketing bonanza for the food franchise as they sold bright orange T-shirts featuring the station's call letters and the slogan "Thirst Quenchers." Letters poured into the station and local newspapers, praising the format. A nerve had been hit, in a good way.

The station broadcast twenty-four hours a day, seven days a week because "man's physical and spiritual needs don't fall only on Sundays or from 6:00 a.m. to midnight," said KBHL creator Larry King, who'd had visions of owning a rock music station ever since he was eighteen years old. When he became a Christian a few years later, he wanted a radio ministry that would touch souls.

The station later got into heavy promotion of concerts. They pushed shows by Barry McGuire, 2nd Chapter of Acts, and others whom Nebraskans would consider stars. (After a few years, though, KBHL ran out of gas and changed its music/program format to country in late 1980 to capitalize on the *Urban Cowboy* phenomenon sweeping America. The running joke in Lincoln was that the call letters now stood for "Keep Buyin' Hog Livers.")

Not to be outdone, Houston, Texas, also debuted its first Christian music station, KFMK ("For My Kingdom"), in 1975. Originally an underground rock station birthed in the late sixties, it was finally yanked off the air when a couple of jocks concocted an on-air stunt that drew the ire of the Federal Communications Corporation. (Its license was pulled after they broadcast the location of a police bust in progress. Authorities, both federal and local, were not amused.) Their hippie loss turned out to be God's gain.

The new KFMK didn't do anything different from the other Christian stations in terms of its format. That was exactly the idea. These pioneering

stations didn't want to go too far out on a limb and chase people away with their ideology or music. To strike a balance, they padded the Jesus Rock with middle-of-the-road songs.

One veteran deejay put it best when he pointed out that the music had to be "not too rock and not too hokey." The radio stations had to navigate slowly to find their way, but it was evidence of a building wave.

And it wasn't just the airwaves. *Harmony*—a professional publication devoted solely to the new sound—took its first bow in 1975. The previous Christian music magazine, *Rock in Jesus*, had debuted in December 1971. It lasted only five issues until it morphed into *Right On!* and then later as an insert in a college newspaper.

Harmony was in the planning stages for almost a year. The timing was particularly fortuitous for editor Dan Hickling, who had been laid off from the Ford Motor Company plant in Buffalo, New York, before being hired by publishers Lou and Peggy Hancherick.

The high-gloss magazine featured interviews with major Christian artists and carried record reviews and tour information. It was well-received by almost everyone in the Christian entertainment world, fans included.

"It was almost a full-time job just trying to find out what was happening in

BARRY MCGUIRE PERFORMING ON STAGE AT CREATION FEST '79.

Jesus Music," Hickling said. "Until 1975 we hardly had any communication from the record companies. I wanted *Harmony* to be a forum for information and exchange of ideas between artists and others involved in contemporary Christian ministries."

Sadly, *Harmony* could not gain enough traction, and financially, the publishers couldn't make a go of it. Its doors were shuttered after fourteen months.

As crucial as these magazines were to what would later be known as Contemporary Christian music, they had the same problems radio initially had: They all existed only in their silos. No one outside of their area knew of their existence. These two publications were important because they were the first of their kind. Others—like *Gospel Trade*, *Contemporary Christian Music* magazine, *Cornerstone Magazine*, and *Straight Magazine*—would later follow suit and become successful by becoming bigger and bolder, and by going national.

An industry began to bubble up. In April 1975, a group of Christian producers, engineers, publishers, concert promoters, theater groups, record company executives, managers, ministers,

A NERVE HAD BEEN HIT, IN A GOOD WAY.

broadcasters, songwriters, and artists decided that the left hand had to know what the right hand was doing and made a concerted effort to improve communications.

The twenty or so charter members met in Fort Wayne, Indiana, to form a national organization named the Fellowship of Contemporary Christian Ministries (FCCM) to provide a forum for creativity, learning, and fellowship for young artists, coffeehouses, and concert promoters in the aftermath of the Jesus Movement. They also held an annual conference to discuss trends in the business, share victories and failures with each other, network, and discover ways in which they could build their industry and enhance their ministries.

"The FCCM was born out of a desire to see the segmented ministries of the contemporary outreaches brought together under a common mode of communication and fellowship," said Paul Craig Paino Jr., a minister at Calvary Temple in Fort Wayne who called for the meeting.

These radio stations, magazines, and the FCCM all needed one thing to help them truly break out: a breakout star.

No one knew it, but their breakout star was preparing for exactly that in a Nashville church.

All of them were about to launch into the stratosphere.

CHAPTER 6

FROM DIRT TO DOLLARS

The 1980s became the golden era for Christian music.

The hippie-driven Jesus Movement came to an abrupt end, and Christian music exploded. The growing pains of the previous decade were mostly over.

Albums, broad store distribution, festivals, and promotion all came together and created an industry. The moneylenders suddenly entered

nation's 8,240 radio stations played Christian music; Christian acts were making enough money to actually quit their day jobs.

Major labels like Warner Brothers, CBS, and MCA joined the act. They all had Christian subsidiary labels, and their products began appearing in major outlets. Was payola involved? Probably yes. Only God knows.

These records didn't sell in the millions like

FROM DIRT TO DOLLARS

the temple . . . and changed everything. Many in the press were quick to point out that "American materialism and spiritual bankruptcy" served as the catalyst behind the explosion of Contemporary Christian music, but in the US, that's what moves the train.

The music business has many tentacles, and by the start of the decade, they had embraced every aspect of Christian music. There were no longer just handful of Christian radio stations, mostly situated in the Bible Belt. Now, approximately 3,000 of the

the Eagles, Led Zeppelin, AC/DC, Pink Floyd, or Foreigner, but they sold decently—in the hundreds of thousands at first—and there was enough profit margin for record companies to deal with.

Rock 'n' roll had *Rolling Stone*, *Hit Parader*, and *Creem*. Christian music needed its own flagship publication to chronicle the phenomenon. Three years after Harmony magazine had launched, it already had twenty thousand subscribers. But album reviews and fan-friendly features like artist profiles were no substitute for a chart. *Contemporary*

Christian Music magazine, started by John Styll in July 1978, ranked the ponies, and readers lined up to put their money behind the winners. Just as everyone in the secular world wanted the biggest hit of the day in *Billboard* magazine, Christian fans and artists weren't any different. The chart not only ranked an act's popularity, but it quantified the growth of the industry. It also gave fans a sense of community. *Billboard* eventually began charting

bin of Christian boutiques or found at a consignment thrift store. They were now on equal footing and could be found in Sam Goody, Wherehouse, and Tower Records.

But there was debate about what belonged in those stores.

Irish rockers U2 came out with their first album, *Boy*, in 1980. Lead singer Bono was vocal about his faith, but the band was adamant about

Christian artists as well, though they called it "Inspirational Music." But that label was uninspired and didn't capture what was actually happening.

In reality, the genre had gone from Jesus Music to Christian Pop to what is known formally today as "Contemporary Christian music" or CCM.

What had once been a balkanized hodge-podge was now a brand, a category, and a platform. If you went into a record store asking for CCM, employees knew exactly what you were talking about. Christian records were no longer stuck in the back

not playing CCM. They were called the "greatest Christian band that never was."

That was just as well for some. Lots of people hated crossover bands like U2. Many churches and parishioners began pushing back against Contemporary Christian music for the smallest of reasons.

"It has drums!" was one strident objection.

U2 guitarist "The Edge" was told by a member of his Dublin church that he couldn't be in a band and be a Christian at the same time. Many others,

Contemporary Christian

MAGAZINE

REZ GETS DOWN

KEAGGY'S COMEBACK

CHICAGO-BASED REZ BAND, LED BY GLENN AND
WENDI KAISER, WAS A STAPLE OF THE CHRISTIAN
ROCK SCENE FOR DECADES AND CONSIDERED A
FORERUNNER TO THE CHRISTIAN METAL GENRE.

like pop singer and Christian artist B.J. Thomas, were also getting grief from the faithful. He was often heckled at his concerts and eviscerated by fans for mixing his secular hits and Christian material.

"A lot of my concerts are big and painful experiences for the Christian community," Thomas said. "It's always got to be some kind of Bible cliché or Christian song, or they feel it's their right before God to reject and judge and scoff."

Kerry Livgren, a founding member of the progressive rock band Kansas ("Carry On My Wayward Son" and "Dust in the Wind"), became a Christian, after a hotel room conversion in 1979. Despite how his faith was showing up in his songs, he was scared to death to play outside of secular venues because of "Christian self-righteousness."

"The problem I have with the Christian music circuit is that it brings about a situation where the only people that listen to Christian music are people who are already Christians," Livgren said. "The Bible tells us to come out and be separate, but I don't think that means to cut yourself off from the world."

Even Christian music's golden girl, the wholesome Amy Grant, wasn't immune to criticism. In fact, she bore the brunt of the microscopic, shortsighted carp coming from the religious intelligentsia. Grant was put in a position more familiar to politicians than musicians. She was both wildly popular and incessantly judged for the pettiest perceived transgressions. Looking at her music videos and concert footage three decades later, the first

AMY GRANT'S SEVENTH ALBUM, *UNGUARDED* (1985) SIGNALED THE ARRIVAL OF A SUPER-STAR AND MAINSTREAM ARTIST.

thought that comes to mind is, *How could anyone think this is immoral in any way?* It was like cursing out Snow White or Pippi Longstocking.

When she wore a leopard print coat and went barefoot at her concerts, it was a problem for some. On one album cover, *My Father's Eyes*, the three top buttons on her blouse were unbuttoned. Critics whispered this "wanton display" of flesh caused impure thoughts to rise even though she wore a cross in the picture. In one of her music videos, she appeared with a man who wasn't her husband. (They didn't embrace, or kiss, or have any physical contact; they were simply in the same frame at the same time.) For some, that earned her a scarlet letter.

If none of that horrified her audience, her divorce was still to come.

But Christian acts, both in concert and on album covers, were beginning to veer toward the mainstream more than what the critics had in mind. They closely resembled the top arena acts.

Chicago's REZ band was Christian music's answer to Led Zeppelin, minus Satan, Tolkien, and the blues. Today, they are considered the forerunner to Christian metal, which is akin to taking credit for Jazzercise, leg warmers, and shoulder pads in women's business suits. Servant, a heavy-rocking but faceless band like Foreigner or REO Speedwagon, used familiar staples such as smoke bombs, flash pots, strobe lights, a slideshow, and dry ice in their shows. They had every gimmick except lasers and giant blow-up animals. They were deemed too raucous by church elders and too aggressive to be authentically Christian. Petra was without a doubt CCM's first superstar rock band. These righteous rockers struck a chord with the mainstream, earning them the title of the "world's most popular Christian rock band." Their logo was a golden cross and sword, and they used the latter to execute band members on a regular basis. Petra ended up having as many members as Black Sabbath and the Flying Burrito Brothers. They were particularly hated by televangelist Jimmy Swaggart, who felt they were a "tool of the devil." That was rich considering how later in the decade Swaggart himself was caught with his pants down, embroiled in a sex scandal involving prostitutes. The image of his weeping confession on TV became a visual metaphor for a card-carrying phony.

The 1980s also saw the birth of New Wave in popular music. CCM was not exempt. Andy McCarroll and Moral Support could bop like the New Romantics or The Clash and then seamlessly float into reggae like Bob Marley and the Wailers. The same went for the Daniel Amos band, which

THEY WERE TRULY ON FIRE FOR THE LORD.

according to one critic had "a humorous New Wave touch with a minimum of preaching . . . though they still left no doubts about their orientation."

There was also a sprinkling of Christian punk bands, such as One Bad Pig, The Choir, and 4-4-1. These youths had the rowdy sound and attitude of their secular counterparts, but they didn't vomit onstage every night, slash themselves with razors, trash the Queen, beat fans with guitars, or snort heroin in the bathroom before gigs. They were truly on fire for the Lord; they simply expressed their faith a little differently from traditionalists.

And at these shows, some of the bigger acts began selling their own merchandise. We're talking concert programs, T-shirts, hats, belt buckles, and the hallmark of eighties rock—concert satin jackets. If you had feathered hair and Jordache jeans, you had to have a satin jacket . . . usually with a groovy logo intricately embroidered on the back.

At first, the church voiced as much opposition to Christian concerts as they did to drums creeping into their worship music. Most finally caved because they figured it was better for their kids to get high on Jesus at a concert than on weed in some dimly lit parking lot.

"Some Christian acts do so well because they're safe," said Dan Russell, an agent who booked Christian shows at the time. "If Mom and Dad are going to send their kid to a concert, it might as well be a Christian rock concert."

With big followings came big wins. Artists like Amy Grant, The Imperials, Petra, Twila Paris, and DeGarmo & Key started collecting framed gold albums from their record companies—meaning their albums were selling half a million units or more. Grant's 1982 album *Age to Age* was the first Christian album recorded by a solo artist to receive gold and platinum certifications from the Recording Industry Association of America (RIAA). It spent an unprecedented eighty-five weeks on the Christian album charts and was the only No. 1 album for the entire year of 1983, minting her as the first superstar of CCM.

"I think the reason why Amy was so poised to be the perfect break-out artist for Christian music is that she sings in a very demure kind of style," said John J. Thompson. "It's like, 'If you have a few minutes I'd like to sing you a song if that'd be okay,' which is the way the church, I think . . . liked women. 'If you need to be on stage, just appreciate your place and be humble about it.' Little did they know who she really was, and the talent was forming in her all that time. She was like a Trojan horse and just snuck in."

Grant said it was the time of her life, making music with people she cared about. One of them was musician and songwriter Michael W. Smith, whom she met in early 1981 during the *Age to Age* sessions. She recognized him as a supremely gifted musician and songwriter with an energy level that matched hers.

MICHAEL W. SMITH AND AMY GRANT REHEARSING A SONG DURING THE *AGE TO AGE* SESSIONS. THEY HAVE REMAINED CLOSE FRIENDS FOR ALMOST FOUR DECADES.

DEGARMO & KEY WAS A HIGHLY POPULAR BUT EDGY CHRISTIAN ROCK ACT FORMED BY EDDIE DEGARMO AND DANA KEY IN 1977.

"He'd have an idea, then another idea, then he'd run around, and then had another idea," Grant recalled. "He'd just jump around a lot, and he talked fast. He was so energetic . . . he was really hyper. He was this fire hose of energy."

Smith penned three songs for the *Age to Age* album, which begat a creative partnership and life-long friendship.

"I wouldn't be [where I am today] had it not been for Amy taking this chance on a kid from West Virginia," Smith said.

John J. Thompson said Grant and Smith were akin to the king and queen of the prom of eighties CCM. "If it wasn't for them, I'm not sure where the bar would be," Thompson said.

Another dynamic duo came in the form of DeGarmo & Key, a Christian rock act formed in 1977 by Eddie DeGarmo and Dana Key. They had a signature sound of slickly produced Kenny Loggins-style synth rock, which struck a chord with fans.

They were notable for having the first Christian rock album (*This Ain't Hollywood*) nominated for a Grammy Award and the first American Christian group to have a video ("Six, Six, Six") entered into MTV's rotation. (The video involved a floppy disc and seduction by the devil, which took place in the form of a feather-haired beauty plying the protagonist with red wine while lightning flashes and bystanders turn into skeletons. This was not even scary by 1980s standards.)

Ironically—providentially—a staff writer for a Christian magazine called *Campus Life* discovered DeGarmo & Key. Although they were edgy even for a teenaged audience, thousands of kids from everywhere heard these performers for the first time and loved their music. That staff writer, Stephen R. Lawhead, went on to become an internationally renowned author of fiction, dragging Christian rock to the top right along with him and his acclaim.

MTV banned "Six, Six, Six" because it was deemed "too violent" for the music video channel, which had no problem showing models wearing next to nothing, zombies dancing, and anything by Madonna or Mötley Crüe. You say you want a revolution? Sure, that's fine. Go ahead and call for the downfall of Western civilization. That's cool. But start singing about the resurrection or the mark of the beast, and . . . well, that will get you banned faster than you can sing "Papa Don't Preach" (the bête noire of Planned Parenthood) or Warrant's

"Cherry Pie," which offended basically everyone who wasn't a teenage boy.

But the DeGarmo & Key video was just fine for the White House and the Moral Majority, a political action committee that shelled out millions of dollars to help put Ronald Reagan in office. CCM also aligned perfectly with the era's conservative morals, values, and policies of the Religious Right. CCM was pro-America, pro-family, pro-school prayer, but anti-abortion . . . and they absolutely abhorred commies. Is it any wonder this was the heyday of Stallone, Schwarzenegger, and Chuck Norris? They had no problem whatsoever dropping a nuke on Russia, China, or Iran if they got out of line. Love thine enemy? Sure. But only after vengeance and vindication. Wags joshed that the Moral Majority was neither moral nor a majority. Much like today's

obsession with virtue signaling, the Moral Majority saw Satan's claws in everything.

This subgenre of CCM drifted from "Love Thy Neighbor" to "Blow Your Enemies to Bits." An obsession with rapture theology crept into Contemporary Christian music . . . and it sold!

Rapture theology isn't old. It's a relatively recent doctrine of American evangelical Protestantism. There are slightly different versions, but the basic belief runs along these lines: Dead believers in Christ will be resurrected and ascend to meet the Lord "in the air," then living believers will join them. Seven years of tribulation will follow. (Think war, famine, strife—or the year 2020—and you get the idea.) After that, Christ will return to preside over a thousand-year messianic kingdom, and the final judgment will be issued. You may have seen the bumper sticker: "In case of the rapture this car will be unmanned." It leaked into the music mainly because, especially for metal bands, it was low-hanging fruit—violent, dramatic, passionate, and heavy-handed.

However, Contemporary Christian music acts were grabbing attention, and they were getting a lot of it. With attention comes fame . . . and with fame comes temptation.

WITH ATTENTION COMES FAME ... AND WITH FAME COMES TEMPTATION.

CHAPTER 7

FALLEN ANGELS

After Madonna hit superstardom in the early 1980s, female pop stars sprouted up all over the place. Cyndi Lauper, Sheena Easton, Annie Lennox, Laura Branigan, Whitney Houston, Belinda Carlisle, Sade, and Janet Jackson, to name a few. Contemporary Christian music was no different after Amy Grant broke the sound barrier.

Grant, Sandi Patty, Michael W. Smith, Carman,

You have your screaming crowds, and we have our screaming crowds," he said. "You have your merch, and we have our merch. Sometimes those two worlds of stardom and fame and accountability and godliness collide."

Contemporary Christian music artists started to appear everywhere: radio, television, in concert, and in video thanks to the Trinity Broadcasting Network. In 1983 they began airing a weekly television show

FALLEN ANGELS

Steve Taylor, Keith Green, Rich Mullins, Twila Paris, and Petra—these were the major artists who helped CCM become one of the fastest-growing music genres in America.

In less than a decade, Christian music sales skyrocketed almost 250 percent. Many CCM artists and bands found crossover appeal with both spiritually driven and secular listeners.

It was a mirror image of what happened in pop culture, Greg Laurie noted. "You have your pop stars; we have our Christian pop stars right here.

called *Real Videos*. They finally gave CCM stars a platform to showcase their music videos, providing much-needed exposure to artists like Mylon & Broken Heart, Bash-n-the-Code, Kenny Marks, Sheila Walsh, and a new Christian metal band that was starting to make a lot of noise: Stryper.

The acts signed autographs for fans and hawked albums, T-shirts, and posters. Their fans gobbled it up and bought it all, including a polycarbonate plastic weighing about half an ounce called the compact disc when it was introduced in the spring of 1983. Fans began treating the artists like major celebrities. That posed new problems for these artists of faith.

"Anytime your face gets on a video or gets on CD covers or magazines, you do become larger than life, and I think as Christians . . . we do have a responsibility to keep this in perspective and not to place people on pedestals in an inappropriate way," said John Styll, publisher of *CCM* magazine. "These

Gospel Music Association (GMA) in 1971 because of alleged ballot-stuffing by the Blackwood Brothers Quartet. Apparently, the gospel quartet sold an extraordinary amount of GMA memberships that year, which skewed the final results in their favor. As it turned out, they needed more than the hand of God to win the award.

But the scandal had faded away by the time the awards were first telecast on March 7,

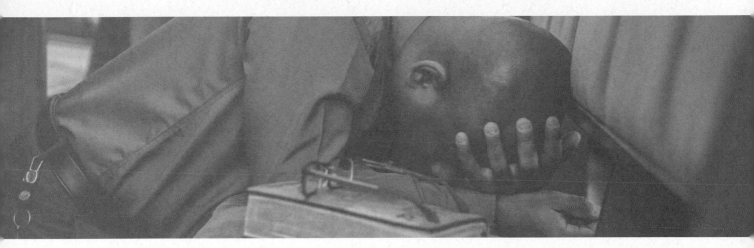

people put their pants on one leg at a time just like everybody else."

True, but that was wisdom dispensed from a veteran journalist trained to view artists objectively and as humans. Adoring fans had a different perspective and elevated them to icon status. The pedestal only got higher when award shows entered the picture.

The Dove Awards, which started in 1969 for gospel artists, was tainted just two years after it started. The awards were deemed invalid by the

1984, at the Tennessee Performing Arts Center in Nashville. The excitement surrounding CCM resulted in an annual showcase of top talent that gave these stars another level of exposure and excitement. The star-studded show included Amy Grant, Sandi Patty, Russ Taff, B.J. Thomas, The Imperials, Al Green, Billy Smiley, Petra, and the Maranatha Singers, who were still clinging to the Jesus sound.

Music sales were big, venues were sold out, merchandising was through the roof, money was

ORIGINATING AS A SOUTHERN GOSPEL QUARTET, THE GRAMMY AND DOVE AWARD-WINNING IMPERIALS ARE CONTEMPORARY CHRISTIAN MUSIC PIONEERS AND MEMBERS OF THE GOSPEL MUSIC HALL OF FAME.

in the equation, and the stars were becoming as big as the projections on the screens behind them.

They were no longer like anyone else.

The industry and the road took artists away from their families and into an alternate reality. Egos grew larger, patience grew thinner, and the strain often became unbearable. Stardom turned out to be the worst possible scenario for a Christian, leading to temptation that eventually chips away at the strongest spiritual armor.

Ken Mansfield, record executive, producer, and Christian author, knew this world well. He was close to the Beatles, the Beach Boys, and other rock luminaries of the 1960s and 1970s. He summed it up this way: "Home and hearth become so far in the distance that you find you can exit and enter alternate lives each time you get on the next chartered airplane and get off at the next town. The warmth of your God-given mate is replaced by the sizzling allure of strangers—wild-eyed fans to whom you don't have to be accountable. All this time you are lost in your sensual gluttony that you think you are the one using them.

"In time the walls of the hotels, lobbies, bars, backstage dressing rooms, unfamiliar places, and phony people start closing in. They become what you wanted them to be: meaningless. And then you begin feeling alone and trapped . . . you keep getting farther away from home, to the point where you don't know if you will ever find your way back. Then you start doing strange things."

John Schlitt, lead singer of Petra, said that humans—and especially Christian artists—are not infallible or immune to sin.

"Satan is so good at what he does, and he never gives up," Schlitt said in 2021. "As humans, we're not perfect. We're not Christ. We're weak. We have egos and insecurities, and we have needs."

The church wanted CCM artists to be road pastors and examples. The audience was often judgmental. Sometimes they saw this new style of music as watering down the message. And they felt it was their God-given right to keep these artists in check with verbal brickbats and condemnations. Showing empathy and the famous Bible verse from Matthew, "Judge not, lest ye be judged," somehow slipped their minds.

It was a different and unenlightened time, according to music historian John J. Thompson. "Back in the 1980s, whenever a Christian artist did anything that leaned toward the mainstream, the church people freaked out," Thompson said. "There's no better way to get arrows in your back than to start looking at the rest of the world. All those arrows came from the church."

Beloved gospel singer Andraé Crouch was one of the first people to receive an arrow in the back. That happened in November 1982 when the Los Angeles police spotted the forty-year-old driving

"ALL THOSE ARROWS CAME FROM THE CHURCH."

erratically on the Marina Freeway and pulled him over.

After a search of the car uncovered drugs, Crouch was arrested and held overnight. He was released after posting $2,500 bail. Ultimately, no charges were pressed. According to Crouch, the coke rocks on the car floor were a diet supplement, specifically a milk powder food for dieters. And the roach in the ashtray was too small an amount for Crouch to be charged. Besides, it wasn't his. He offered the age-old explanation that the skunk weed belonged to a musician friend who was staying at his apartment. Crouch was simply trying to teach him a better way.

Crouch told a reporter he was innocent but did admit to being guilty of "putting too much trust in other people."

He explained a little later to *CCM* magazine that he was getting psychiatric help to get over the trauma. The confession backfired. All it did was make the faithful wonder why a higher power hadn't been sought.

Four years after the incident, he still denied the allegations, ducking the question from a *San Francisco Examiner* reporter who was promoting an upcoming show.

"We don't talk about that at all," Crouch said. "I don't want to inform anybody that didn't already know about it, since it was a lie."

Crouch's reputation was tarnished, and he disappeared from the church for a while. He began

THE LIST OF THOSE WHO SLIPPED ONE WAY OR ANOTHER WAS NOT SHORT.

writing for movies (*The Color Purple* and *The Lion King*) and secular artists such as Michael Jackson, Madonna, Elton John, and Diana Ross. He eventually experienced great success, earning seven Grammy Awards.

He came back to the fold in the 1990s after his parents died and he and his sister took over the Los Angeles church they founded. He was eventually redeemed.

Singer-songwriter Russ Taff's weakness was booze. He had a traumatic childhood filled with angst, guilt, and chaos courtesy of his father, a Pentecostal preacher who was also an alcoholic.

"I got my humor from him. I got my charisma from him," Taff said. "But he wrecked my life. Music was the thing that held me through all those years."

What wrecked him were the harsh things his father told him on a daily basis growing up: "You're not worth the salt that goes on your bread. You're not worth the bullet to shoot yourself with. You'll never amount to anything."

Taff found all the insecurities and voices in his head were quelled when he drank alcohol. He never touched the stuff when he was onstage or rehearsing, but once his business was finished for the day, it waited for him in the dressing or hotel room. That led to addiction.

"My body demanded that I have it every day . . . And it started this journey to hell," Taff said. "Music starts going further and further and further away . . . and it's not that comfort that it used to be. It's not that wonderful place where I could fellowship with God because I hated myself."

The Grammy Award–winning artist was on the verge of a cover story in *CCM* magazine when he had lunch with editor John Styll. During that meal, Taff admitted he had a weakness for alcohol. He said if Styll cut him out of the upcoming issue, he would understand.

"If we were to take everyone out who had a sin problem in their life," Styll deadpanned, "then we'd publish blank paper."

The list of those who slipped one way or another was not short. No handbook existed for pitfalls in the Christian church for these daring musical pioneers and fallen angels, but an ever-changing catalog of sin seemed to rear its head at every turn.

Sure, sin could be forgiven . . . but too much was too much. A wandering eye? Okay. A wandering

AMY GRANT AND HER MUSICAL TEAM ACCEPTING AN AWARD FOR HER WORK. HER SOARING CAREER WOULD FACE CHALLENGES AS DARK TIMES IN HER PERSONAL LIFE BECAME PUBLIC IN THE '90s.

hand? No. One cold beer on the porch on a hot evening? A man might be forgiven for that. But not for showing up at eleven in the morning redolent of vodka fumes.

An extramarital affair or a divorce? Depending on who you were in the Christian music pantheon, it could cost you your career.

Even a megaselling artist like Amy Grant.

Grant had been married to fellow Christian musician Gary Chapman since 1982. They had three kids and a seemingly picture-perfect life. Things in their marriage started to change in late 1993 when Grant accepted country star Vince Gill's invitation to appear with him on a Christmas special in Tulsa, Oklahoma.

"We got along like two peas in a pod and made no bones about it," Grant said to *Tennessean* reporter Jay Orr.

As their friendship grew and deepened, others began to whisper.

Grant and Chapman's marriage had been rocky for some time. They sought counseling as early as 1986. Compounding their problems was the fact that Chapman developed a cocaine and marijuana habit—a coping mechanism for living in Grant's "awesome shadow," he told one reporter.

Things got ugly when Chapman starting talking more regularly to the press.

"A lot of disparaging things were said of my very public friendship with Vince," Grant said. "I don't take lightly the responsibility of being a public person, of my faith, all of those things. I know why God hates divorce because it's painful and it's hardest on the kids and you have to kiss your history goodbye, start over."

Six years later she filed for divorce from Chapman, citing irreconcilable differences. She might as well have thrown a grenade at her audience.

Christian radio stations quit playing her music, and Christian bookstores pulled her albums.

The scarlet letter she earned for appearing in a music video with another man a few years earlier just got painted bright red. She was being canceled.

"The Christian community felt like they owned Amy. 'She's ours, and we are hers,'" John Styll said. "So for her marriage to fail or for what they considered for her to have a moral failing, was a bridge too far for some people . . . it hurt her career."

It took almost three years and multiple mea culpas in publications like *CCM* magazine and the *Tennessean* to rehabilitate her characteristically virtuous image.

"I never thought I would wind up here. I look at the choices all along the way that were made and think, I did the very best I could, and I wound up here, now," Grant said. "I want to stand up and say, 'It's not the way you think it was!' But it doesn't really matter."

Megastar Michael W. Smith said it can get confusing when the church gives a Christian artist the cold shoulder and you watch a friend struggle.

"I DID THE VERY BEST I COULD, AND I WOUND UP HERE, NOW."

"If there's anything dark about the church on some level [it] is how judgmental we've been. You just feel like, 'Where's the love?'" Smith said. "It was hard for me to watch. You have a great friend that hurts, and you hurt too."

They were dark times, indeed. Perhaps no one was harder on Grant than herself. She recalled drawing a lonely cabin that was overgrown with weeds.

"I couldn't even find a path to it . . . I think somewhere in there the cabin was probably me," Grant said recently. "You lose yourself. You lose your way, your integrity. You find that you have lied. You let people down. I took this drawing, and I wrote, 'I think I have forfeited every right that I ever had to be on the stage.'"

The same sword that almost beheaded Amy Grant fell on Sandi Patty, whose squeaky-clean image made Grant look like Madonna. So when it came out that the reason behind Patty's breakup of her marriage was infidelity with one of her backup singers, Don Peslis (a man she later married), she got what was tantamount to an Old Testament stoning by evangelical America.

Her 1993 divorce from her manager, John Helvering, stunned the industry and her adoring fans, who dubbed her "The Voice." Already a five-time Grammy winner who had also racked up an astounding twenty-nine Dove Awards, Patty's career was soaring like an eagle. American Christendom's public bastion of family values was in good hands

SANDI PATTY PUBLICLY ADMITTED HER MORAL FAILINGS AND SPENT A FEW YEARS OUT OF THE LIMELIGHT BEFORE RETURNING TO MUSIC. SHE WAS INDUCTED INTO THE GOSPEL MUSIC HALL OF FAME IN 2004.

MICHAEL ENGLISH WAS ASKED TO GIVE HIS DOVE AWARDS BACK IN 1994. HE WOULD EVENTUALLY SPEAK OPENLY ABOUT HIS FALL FROM GRACE AND FINDING HIS WAY BACK.

with this soprano who even sang a concept album on children, parenthood, and family. Her sleeping with another man for seventeen months—a married one at that—was too much. Her apple pie fanbase dropped her like a hot potato.

By now it doesn't take much imagination to guess her punishment: the usual litany of twentieth-century flagellation and hair shirts. Tours were canceled. Product was removed from shelves. Christian stations stopped spinning her records, and bags of hate mail appeared on her doorstep. She read them too. At least Twitter didn't exist yet.

Like for Grant, it took a few years before her career momentum swung back.

"I had an affair, and that was wrong. I was not honest, and that was wrong," Patty said in a 1995 interview with *CCM* magazine. "As I have grown in the last three or four years and felt like my life was coming closer to the Lord, there were things I had to deal with. One was go to the people and be honest, not only about the affair but to be honest about not being honest."

That was only one of the interviews she gave on her contrition circuit. There were many others, plus an autobiography (*Broken on the Back Row*), before the public bloodlust had been slaked and she could go back to making music. She had done everything but renounce a worldly life and retire to a convent. The drama was over.

Men weren't exempt from judgment either.

"WE ALL NEED ACCOUNTABILITY AND BARRIERS IN OUR LIFE."

Christian recording artist Michael English was forced to give up his four Dove Awards in May 1994 after admitting to an extramarital affair with Marabeth Jordan, a long-haired, dark-eyed brunette and a member of the Christian group First Call, who recorded and toured with the superstar.

Ironically, it was a tour to benefit unwed mothers. Jordan soon found herself pregnant by English, and their affair caused wreckage far beyond what anyone could have imagined. Both were married, just to other people.

The two parties told their respective spouses they had been violating the seventh commandment, which went over about as well as a devil worshipper at one of their concerts. Then someone leaked the information to English's record label, Warner Alliance. English wanted them and his management team to support him, but they told him that wasn't possible. From there, his life spiraled.

After English sent back his awards, he was dropped by Warner Alliance, who forced him to make a public apology to his fans. He did so, begrudgingly. Christian music stores removed his albums from their bins, and radio stations stopped playing his songs. Overnight, English went from prince to pariah. English claims the Christian music industry turned its back on him.

English left the scene for a while and ended up divorcing his wife. Jordan was given the pink slip by her group and, shortly after their relationship became public, miscarried the child she and English had conceived.

Soon, English was in full prodigal mode: He fell away from the CCM industry, developed a $400-a-day pill habit (painkillers were his poison of choice), and entered into a series of relationships with women. He got to a place where he was essentially homeless and ran out of money due to drugs.

"I had exhausted every avenue trying to support the drug habit that I had," English told a reporter from *Reuters*. "I was selling anything and everything that I could find that was worth anything on eBay. I didn't have a voice. I couldn't sing anymore. I lost my reputation, my life, my family, my finances, my home, and my voice, so I had nothing."

Sensing English was in need, his old friend and employer Bill Gaither reached out in March 1999 to give him a hand up. He invited English to appear at a recording of *Gaither Homecoming*. This was followed by English's 2000 solo album, *Heaven to Earth*. English

"YOUNG PEOPLE LOOK UP TO THEM AS HEROES."

used promotional efforts for that album to share his testimony about his fall from grace and battle with drugs. It brought him in good standing once again with Christian audiences, but he sure was humbled.

Christian music fans and the church aren't as empathetic or understanding as they should be according to Al Andrews, who heads up the Nashville-based program Porter's Call, which counsels artists from all genres.

"I think Christian artists versus country, rock, and pop face the same challenges, but their audience is different," Andrews said. "This is really going to be strange, but the country audience, the pop audience, is more forgiving."

Greg Laurie said, to be fair, Christians expected these artists not only to sing about their faith, but also to live by it.

"People are not looking for perfection, but they are looking for authenticity and personal integrity. Young people look up to them as heroes," Laurie said. "The problem is the 'star-making machinery' was

impacting the artists in CCM in a similar way as its secular counterpart.

"Take a person away from their family, their church and send them on endless tours . . . [this] cannot end all that well even for the strongest believer. We all need accountability and barriers in our life."

Personal pitfalls were usually a man-versus-himself conflict. But there was a man-versus-man conflict brewing in CCM, and it was about to get a lot uglier. A religious war loomed.

AS A HIGHLY INFLUENTIAL AND RESPECTED ARTIST, RICH MULLINS STAYED HONEST ABOUT HIS QUESTIONS AND STRUGGLES. IN 1997 HE DIED IN A TRAGIC CAR ACCIDENT AT THE AGE OF FORTY-ONE.

CHAPTER 8

THE ROCK WARS

The metal scene erupted. That meant the arrival of a few things the world had to get used to regarding their newly minted rock stars: an overabundance of teased hair, mascara, multiple tattoos, leather vests, studded belts, spiked wristbands, tight spandex, red bandanas, and the flashing of horns—the official salute of the Sunset Strip.

"The metal scene in the eighties, man . . . them), and traded clothes and makeup with their model girlfriends. They partied so hard they made their sixties and seventies rock predecessors look like pikers.

A reading of the 2001 book *The Dirt* by Mötley Crüe will bear this out. It is a primer for indecent behavior and wretched excess in a decade of extreme decadence. When one finishes the book, multiple showers are usually required and so, perhaps, is a

THE ROCK WARS

was decadent," said John J. Thompson. "MTV had launched, and now teenagers are watching music on television, and popular culture and music sales just explodes."

It was loud. It was radical. And it was a free-for-all.

These rockers, most of them barely out of their teens, lived like Caesars for the short time they ruled the music world. They engaged in immoral sex, took illicit drugs, swilled top-shelf booze, bought expensive sports cars (and usually wrecked

blessing from a priest, preferably the Pope. Go forth and sin no more.

But the Joker needs Batman. Almost in lock-step with the rise of Christian metal was the rise of 1980s televangelists. We're talking Jim and Tammy Bakker, Oral Roberts, Kenneth Copeland, Jerry Falwell, Pat Robertson, Rex Humbard, and Paul and Jan Crouch. The latter, who sported a blond and purple Maltese-style wig with ribbons, looked like she could have easily fit in with these metal rockers.

The ones who complained the loudest were Bill Gothard, Jerry Falwell, and David Wilkerson.

Bill Gaither said Jerry Falwell once prodded him about the lifestyle and decadence of some of these Christian rock artists, asking if what he was hearing was true.

"I said, 'Probably are . . . Jerry, if you're looking for me to get a roomful of unflawed artists, it's probably not going to happen,'" Gaither recalled. "I

"Satan always goes too far in his greed to steal and to kill and to destroy," Swaggart said on one of his telecasts. "He gets too perverted, too damnable, too dastardly, so he changes course and then millions fall for it all over again. And today it's called—listen carefully—Christian rock music."

Ironically, Jimmy's cousin, Jerry Lee Lewis, was a musical pioneer who, along with Elvis Presley,

said, 'These are human beings who have been gifted in a special kind of way, and they're trying to work through it in these earthly bodies, and sometimes they make mistakes.'"

But none of them were louder or more consistent in their condemnation than televangelist Jimmy Swaggart, who even wrote a book on the subject. Called *Religious Rock 'n' Roll: A Wolf in Sheep's Clothing*, it was a jeremiad against Contemporary Christian music—a declaration of war.

Little Richard, Carl Perkins, and Johnny Cash, set the whole rock scene into motion.

Swaggart and other opposing evangelists thought Contemporary Christian music was evil because it had a spirit of immorality, divisiveness, and deception, and it set an atmosphere of the church service they didn't like.

Swaggart's list of grievances touched on almost every genre and artist involved with CCM. He disliked the length of Mylon LeFevre's hair and noted that Leslie Phillips was overtly sexual by exposing

PETRA WAS ONE OF THE BIGGEST ACTS IN CONTEM-
PORARY CHRISTIAN MUSIC, ROUTINELY SELLING OUT
CONCERT HALLS AND ARENAS IN THE 1980S AND 1990S.

her stomach onstage. He felt Michael W. Smith's music dominated the message, complained about Undercover's "punk looks and ragged rock sounds," thought Philip Bailey's duo with Phil Collins on "Easy Lover" promoted promiscuity, and opined that Bash-n-the-Code sported an androgynous look and made music compelling listeners toward the dance floor. Swaggart also gave Amy Grant two tallies for being too sensual and not giving altar calls at her concerts.

The subject of modern CCM quickly became fodder for evangelical conferences, where the music was dissected and evil or the devil was seen in every lyric. But what they missed was that this was music for the new generation and attracted young followers just as the Jesus Movement had done a decade before. It was a viable tool for communicating the gospel, but they didn't see it that way at all.

According to John J. Thompson, Christian metal was perceived as the underbelly of the Contemporary Christian music industry. "Christian metal wasn't part of the pie of CCM music. And under that pie was a plate. And under that plate there was a table. And under that table there was a floor. And under that floor was a basement. And under that basement there was a crypt. And in that crypt there were Christian metal bands," Thompson said.

The CCM jungle contained solo acts, duos, trios, and groups in every configuration. Christian rock and metal bands, for all the grief they got, were undoubtedly the kings of the jungle. They sold out arenas, their albums topped charts, and they led the most people to the Lord. Better yet, some of them had more explosions and flamethrowers than Mötley Crüe.

The first of these bands to break through were REZ, Petra, Whiteheart, Jerusalem, Mylon & Broken Heart, and the most significant of the lot, Stryper.

"The established church wanted no part of it," said *Contemporary Christian Music* publisher John Styll. "It was guilty by association with that evil rock 'n' roll."

Whether the music was Christian at all was not debated in the church.

"It was brand-new, and it would be fair to say the discussion wasn't, 'Was this music good or not,' but the question was, 'How can this be Christian music?'" said CCM artist Steve Taylor, who later produced the hugely successful bands Newsboys and Sixpence None the Richer.

But for young people, the draw was experiencing the Lord in their own language according to John Cooper, lead singer of Skillet.

"If you've ever heard of people saying that Christian rock was from the pits of hell, that's the family I grew up in," Cooper said. "My parents would rather me have gone to jail for murder than for me to become a singer."

Cooper did, in fact, become a singer, and his group redefined Christian metal in the late 1990s and early 2000s and has kept the spirit alive through their music, attitude, and sound.

It wasn't just the metal bands. No one would ever accuse DeGarmo & Key of being a metal band, but they didn't have it any easier than the spandex crowd.

"The church didn't really accept us. It took us, in the early days of Christian music, a lot of thick skin to make it through that," DeGarmo said. "I mean, I had tomatoes thrown at me, man. I'm thankful it wasn't rocks."

The bigger the act, the bigger the target. And there was no bigger CCM act than Petra in the 1980s. They were routinely drawing twenty thousand fans a night with their arena tours, competing right along with the likes of rockers Journey, REO Speedwagon, and Ozzy Osbourne. They were Christian rock's first breakout group.

DEGARMO & KEY HAVING A LITTLE FUN WHILE ROCKING OUT ON STAGE.

THE BIGGER THE ACT, THE BIGGER THE TARGET.

"Petra was the first band I heard, and I thought, *Oh my gosh, what is this?*" said CCM artist Chris Tomlin. "I think I was in sixth grade or fifth grade. I was like, 'I love this.' That rock 'n' roll kind of thing to Christian music . . . I thought, *Wow!*"

John Cooper was also pumped up when he first heard Petra. He was so excited that a Christian band could rock so hard in the name of Jesus that he just had to share the music with his mother.

Big mistake.

"My mom gave me the holiest butt whooping a parent has ever given a child," Cooper said.

That was nothing compared to what Petra got from the church.

It was disheartening for singer John Schlitt, who left seventies rockers Head East at the end of the decade after a life of excess. After contemplating suicide, he had a born-again experience. Joining Petra fit his new outlook. He figured that the band's main battle was going to be with the secular music world not accepting them. He was surprised to discover the real enemies were misguided televangelists and the church system.

"I thought that the Christian side of things would be welcoming and welcoming us with open arms. And the truth is it was totally reversed," Schlitt said. "The world basically said, 'Petra are good musicians.' But what freaked me out, what surprised me the most, was we would play in one church and there was another church picketing us outside of the building in the parking lot, basically saying we were from hell. That we were Satanists."

Schlitt recalled a night in Greenville, North Carolina, when the band tried to recruit a group of picketers to help them with the altar call, thinking

seeing them in action might change their opinion. They came inside, stood with their arms folded, and did nothing.

"They didn't help one bit, walked out and not one mind was changed," Schlitt said. "They walked in with an attitude and walked out with an attitude. And no matter what we did, it was how they were taught, and this was how it was going to be."

Petra's altar calls numbered in the thousands. One night they reached an astounding ten thousand souls. Their albums routinely sold between half a million and a million copies. Despite their success, the band fought opposing attitudes for years and years. Schlitt still gets questions asking

JOHN COOPER OF SKILLET HELPED TO REDEFINE THE SOUND OF METAL IN THE 1990S. DESPITE COMING FROM A FAMILY THAT CONDEMNED CHRISTIAN ROCK MUSIC, HE WAS PROFOUNDLY IMPACTED BY HIS FAVORITE JESUS ROCKERS.

him what he thinks about people who say you can't have Christian rock. He doesn't say a thing to them.

"I ignore them because I'm not doing it for them. I'm doing it for Christ," Schlitt said. "I'm the one that has to face him when it's time. I don't care what these people are saying. They've been taught the way they've been taught. They've been brainwashed the way they've been brainwashed, and it's not my problem. It's theirs."

THIS MEANS WAR!, PETRA (1987, STARSONG RECORDS) WAS A ROCK ALBUM WITH A GOSPEL MESSAGE AND CATCHY TUNES.

That's how he looks at it now. He wishes he looked at it that way in the beginning because it really disturbed him that people thought he was from hell. It got to the point where no matter what they did, no matter what God had put on their hearts and how they were being used, it didn't matter. He finally thought, *I don't need to deal with this anymore.*

The turning point came when their praise and worship album, *This Means War*, came out in 1987. Some people finally started listening to the lyrics. They found they really loved the commitment to spiritual warfare. And that's when the church started taking them seriously and listening. That was a peak for the band.

"I remember standing in a third-story window at a music theater where we [were] playing. We looked out in the parking lot, and it was packed full of church buses with their youth groups," Schlitt

IN THEIR SIGNATURE YELLOW AND BLACK, STRYPER WAS INSTANTLY RECOGNIZABLE. THEY SHREDDED GUITARS AND PREACHED THE GOSPEL TO ANYONE WHO WOULD LISTEN, CHRISTIANS AND NONBELIEVERS ALIKE.

said. "In other words, all these churches finally trusted us."

Stryper had all the impact of the vengeful Old Testament God. They seemed easily capable of hauling you up to the mountaintop and sacrificing you. They dressed like killer bees, whipped Bibles at their fans, and slayed a lot of demons.

They also put on a heck of a show.

"Stryper had such a theatrical mindset. Every second of their performance was so thought out and so intentional. You were always seeing something new," said Joel Smallbone of for KING & COUNTRY, one of the most successful CCM acts today. "If you look at for KING & COUNTRY, it's basically Stryper."

The band's skills and stage presence were flawless, and they had tons of swagger. This was no Sandi Patty and Larnelle Harris concert. They came through just as strong on TV.

"Stryper comes on [television] and honestly you would have thought it was a satanic killing ritual or something," said Skillet's John Cooper. "My mom was like, 'In the name of Jesus, get to your room!' She then prayed over me."

Stryper tours, despite the outward appearance, were all about reaching people in need and saving souls. They did a number on Ken Mansfield, the music executive and producer who worked with esteemed artists such as the Beatles, Waylon Jennings, Willie Nelson, and David Cassidy. In 1985, Mansfield was at a spiritual crossroads in his life. He once followed an Indian guru, but his Christian fiancée, Connie (later his wife), tried to teach him a better way. She even took him to a few Christian concerts by Mylon & Broken Heart, Rich Mullins, and Petra. But none had the impact of Stryper.

STRYPER
"Always There For You"
HOLLYWOOD

"They had a big part in my conversion because I was blown away seeing a giant venue packed with young people raising their hands and taking part of powerful worship," Mansfield recalled in 2021. "The last time before this when I was in an audience of young people at a heavy rock concert they were stoned, and there was a heavy feeling in the place even though the place was rocking out. With Stryper, there was lightness and tears of joy. Everyone was smiling and a sense of embracing as one the heart of God in fellowship. I realized that is what I wanted from music from then on—a sense of being uplifted, encouraged, and filled with unity and good purpose. Now, I was in my late forties at the time and ironically was seated next to a lady close to my age. She saw how moved I was and reacting, so at the end of the show she introduced herself. She was the mother of Michael and Robert Sweet [brothers and cofounders of Stryper]."

Musician and pastor Michael Guido accompanied Stryper on their first tour, mostly to provide spiritual guidance and protection. They prayed over everything—the car that took them to the venues, the instruments they played, the venue that hosted them, and the hotels where they rested.

Guido saw strange things happen at their shows—satanic inscriptions, demonic possession, lights crashing and barely missing band members' heads, and the power of darkness trying to put a halt to the tour.

"Demons, worshippers, covens, and people would try and interrupt," Guido said.

But Stryper always prevailed. How could they not? They pelted their fans—and music critics—with Bibles.

"I see them at a show, and they're chucking Bibles, and one of them hits me in the face," said John J. Thompson. "What's more Christian than getting hit in the face by a Bible?"

And it wasn't all showmanship.

"The thing about them is they were actually good," said John Styll.

That's because the band's leader, Robert Sweet, was known as a perfectionist and drove the band to be the best and the most evangelistic crossover band in all of Christian music history.

Ironically, Sweet's inspiration came from Jimmy Swaggart.

His older brother drew the entire family into watching the televangelist, whose sermons were like watching a storm on television—all fury and drama.

After one broadcast, the entire Sweet family bowed their heads, repeated the Sinner's Prayer, and accepted Christ in front of the television.

"Literally, Jimmy pretty much became our pastor," Sweet recalled.

This decision impacted not only Sweet's life, but also his band, which included his brother Robert, Oz Fox, and Tim Gaines. They were rockers

"THINGS WERE HAPPENING. IT WAS HUMBLING AND MIRACULOUS."

STRYPER'S *SOLDIERS UNDER COMMAND* (1985), WAS THE FIRST CHRISTIAN METAL ALBUM CERTIFIED GOLD BY THE RIAA.

who became Christians. Instead of changing their look and hair and burning all of their albums in the backyard, they changed their lyrics.

They zigged when everyone else zagged. They wore their hair long, donned black and yellow spandex, and looked every inch the Sunset Strip rocker. But Stryper wasn't just some cheesy imitation; they were the real deal. They even crossed over on a hallowed music network, something not afforded to other Christian bands.

While Stryper got their first airplay on MTV in 1985, the band was used to executives saying they couldn't play their videos because their music had too much Jesus in the lyrics, they were too patriotic, or whatever the excuse of the day happened to be. Then the network created "Dial MTV," and it was no longer up to the program managers; it was up to the fans.

They crushed every other band in the countdown, including acts like Mötley Crüe, Poison, and Bon Jovi.

"Things were happening. It was humbling and miraculous," Sweet recalled. "It didn't happen

WHO IS R.K. FRASER ANYWAY?

Contemporary Christian
MAGAZINE

MYLON'S METHOD OF MODERN MINISTRY

DALLAS HOLM

MYLON LEFEVRE WAS A FAVORITE TARGET OF EVANGELIST JIMMY SWAGGART, WHO DID HIS BEST TO SABOTAGE THE SINGER'S CAREER.

The Singing LeFevres and The Stamps Quartet in the 1960s and then pursued rock 'n' roll in the 1970s. He toured with the likes of Eric Clapton, Elton John, and Billy Joel. The lifestyle caught up with him, and he eventually became a drug addict. He had a near-fatal heroin overdose in 1973, and seven years later he rededicated himself to Christ at a 2nd Chapter of Acts concert.

LeFevre was the perfect template of a rock musician. Tall and thin with jet-black hair hanging over his shoulders, he sported muttonchops in an ode to another Southern rocker, Elvis Presley, who admired LeFevre and recorded one of his songs. He even wore jumpsuits like The King, showing off his chest hair and cross.

He, too, was called out by Swaggart on television.

"Jimmy was holding up this magazine, a *Contemporary Christian Music* magazine. He basically said, 'There's no anointing in that kind of music,'" LeFevre said. "I got my glasses . . . to see who it was, and it was me!"

LeFevre met with Swaggart in person, and they went at it for five hours. LeFevre was crushed when he walked out of the meeting.

"Rejection from the world is no big deal," LeFevre said. "Rejection from the church? This is your family."

It didn't stop there. LeFevre's name appeared in Swaggart's anti-rock book no less than thirty-six times. The televangelist had such disdain for the rocker that he hired a kind of "kill squad" to go

to other bands. There was something going on with Stryper that I can't explain other than God really blessing the band."

Then the evangelists, led by none other than Jimmy Swaggart, crashed their party.

"Once the band made it, that's when we started watching Jimmy [Swaggart] hold up our albums and saying, 'This band right here—Stryper—they're of the devil. They're wolves in sheep's clothing,'" Sweet said. "And we would watch that and think, 'My God.' It hurt because to me he was like family. He was instrumental in saving me, saving my family. I was in tears, man."

Mylon LeFevre was another big target of Swaggart's. He started off in Southern gospel with

"REJECTION FROM THE CHURCH? THIS IS YOUR FAMILY."

after LeFevre's act. They waited in every town and protested the venues where LeFevre appeared in concert. It had a chilling effect on his career. His shows had drawn a few thousand. With Swaggart's targeted attacks, it became a fraction of that.

"People were quitting the band because we couldn't pay them," LeFevre said. "Forgiving those people . . . you have to count the cost in order to truly forgive."

The vitriol and assaults didn't let up for years and had lasting effects on the artists. Stryper's Michael Sweet said he and the group began rebelling against the church, and even God. He also began to drink. He felt that when his family started suffering, it was time to leave. And he did in 1992.

Despite the heartbreak and brickbats from televangelists and even, perhaps, well-meaning church leaders, these radical rockers never really got their due when it came to delivering a gospel message. They sold millions of albums, performed for hundreds of thousands of fans, and led more kids to the Lord than many of their critics.

Contemporary Christian music executive Stan Moser saw this with clarity. "In my view, music is simply a tool, a conduit. Christian music can, has, and will continue to carry the message of Jesus,"

Moser observed. "And in spite of many efforts to discredit Christian rock groups—D&K, REZ, Petra, Mylon & Broken Heart, and Stryper—they did deliver the message of Jesus to a growing number of fans that desperately needed to hear the truth in a language they could understand."

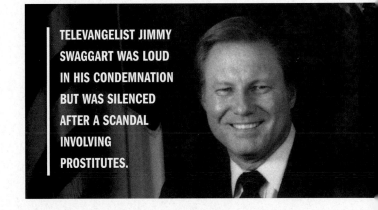

TELEVANGELIST JIMMY SWAGGART WAS LOUD IN HIS CONDEMNATION BUT WAS SILENCED AFTER A SCANDAL INVOLVING PROSTITUTES.

Eventually, Jimmy Swaggart would discredit himself in ways far worse than his criticisms of the alleged doings of Christian rock bands. There was poetic justice in that, as the swaggering Swaggart was so quick to judge others for their alleged sins. The prostitute scandals knocked him off the high perch he had been sitting on for years, humbling him as his ministry and influence shrank dramatically.

As Jimmy Swaggart's cousin Jerry Lee Lewis once sang, there was "a whole lotta shakin' going on."

CHAPTER 9

BOOMTOWN

f Contemporary Christian music rocketed off in the eighties, then the booster was perfected in the nineties.

By this time the proper channels had been in place for more than a dozen years. Distribution pipelines were established. Big-box and retail outlets now carried the product. Record labels earnestly promoted their artists, and radio stations gave listeners everything they

the business competitiveness to these bigger-than-life egos and personalities" said Bill Reeves, CEO of K-LOVE. "Definitely the competition was very fierce."

Musical acts like Amy Grant, Steven Curtis Chapman, Michael W. Smith, Rich Mullins, and Sandi Patty were not only giants of CCM but also had become crossover artists, entering the rarefied air of superstardom. Some of them signed with major

BOOMTOWN

wanted, boosting record companies and artists at the same time.

"It was just this wide-open canvas," Phil Joel of the Newsboys said about the music of the 1990s. "You had grunge, and you had the pop thing. You had rock, and you had hip-hop, just this hodge-podge of creativity going on around the world. Music was at an all-time high."

All the music genres were expanding, and the industry was firing on all cylinders. "It was everything from the spiritual competitiveness to

secular labels like A&M, Geffen, Sony, Capitol, or one of their subsidiaries, hoping their PR muscle would launch them into the stratosphere. And it did.

Platinum albums were no longer the gold standard; artists were selling multiple millions of records. Amy Grant's 1991 album *Heart in Motion* sold five million units thanks to the push by her mainstream label, A&M. The album reached the Top 10 on the *Billboard* 200 charts and spent thirty-two weeks on top of the Christian albums chart. Its lead single, "Baby, Baby," which reached the No. 1

position on the Adult Contemporary chart, played a big role in making *Heart in Motion* the best-selling Christian album of all time. It also played on mainstream radio, MTV, and VH1.

Grant had been enjoying mainstream success for some time. She sang a duet called "Next Time I Fall" with former Chicago lead singer Peter Cetera and zoomed straight to the top of the charts in 1986. She also made an appearance on *The Tonight Show*

like we were part of the vibrant music community. And it wasn't just CCM. It was the world of music. It was just beautiful to be a part of it."

Not everyone felt that way. Many in CCM didn't want Grant to cross over into the mainstream because they were oddly possessive of their acts, recalled John J. Thompson.

"I remember there being a lot of people inside the Christian music world that were trying to make

Starring Johnny Carson, charming the legendary host and making him laugh several times. Most astoundingly, she sold out the Los Angeles Forum on one of her tours—a feat only matched by the likes of Led Zeppelin, Paul McCartney and Wings, the Eagles, Rod Stewart, and Van Halen in their heydays.

"Old dividing walls between genres were getting knocked down," noted Amy Grant. "There was so much great music going on everywhere. Everything felt so fresh and new, like it mattered. We truly felt

that record ["Baby, Baby"] fail," Thompson said. "I mean, arrows were flying."

When music executive Mike Blanton played "Baby, Baby" for Eddie DeGarmo over the telephone and asked him for his reaction, DeGarmo recalled: "I said, 'You know, it's a really good song, and it's really catchy . . . you're really going to catch a lot of hell. Some people are going to understand it, probably more people are going to go with you, but there will be a minority of people, usually with very loud voices, that will oppose you.'"

Singer-songwriter Natalie Grant viewed this as ironic. "God forbid they have a song that the world loves," Grant said. "Did we actually miss the part where we're supposed to go into all of the world and make disciples? But oh my gosh, you didn't say 'Jesus' enough times."

The criticism made Michael W. Smith want to duke it out with the critics for hurting his friend.

"I could tell that it was sort of weighing on her," Smith said. "Sometimes I'd go into her dressing room and sit. Sometimes I wouldn't say anything or say, 'I'm praying for you. It's going to be okay. It doesn't matter what those people think.'"

Despite the flak, other CCM acts were starting to enjoy the same crossover appeal as Grant in the early 1990s. They were interviewed by Oprah Winfrey, Jay Leno, Conan O'Brien, and Regis Philbin, and they hosted their own specials on major networks like the American Broadcasting Corporation (ABC) and VH1. Michael W. Smith made *People* magazine's "Most Beautiful People" list. A lot of CCM acts started to perform at Disneyland, Six Flags, and the White House. Some endorsed political candidates, while others were awarded honorary doctorate degrees at major universities. A few showed up in television and movie parts.

"Today, it's a different world than it was in 1990 or 1992," said Michael W. Smith almost three

SIXPENCE NONE THE RICHER, SELF-TITLED ALBUM (1997, SQUINT). THE ALBUM AND ITS SMASH HIT, "KISS ME," WERE NOMINATED FOR GRAMMY AWARDS.

decades later, whose "Place in This World" from the platinum album *Go West Young Man* reached No. 6 on the *Billboard* Hot 100 singles chart and won a GMA Dove Award for Song of the Year in 1992.

He remembered being at his parents' house when the single was first released, and he received a life-changing phone call.

"I don't remember who called me, but they said, 'Hey, your record just sold 128,000 records in the first week.' I said, 'Yeah, right . . . whatever.' I thought someone was messing with me," Smith said. "All of a sudden this record ["Place in This World"] is being played all over the world. What that song did for me was put me in a whole different category and [with] a whole different audience I actually longed to be with. It broke me out of this genre we called Christian music and got a hit song on pop radio. That was incredible for me. And to be able to drive down the interstate and to turn on the pop station and hear my song."

He also received a grudgingly respectful concert review from the *Los Angeles Times*, a courtesy rarely afforded to Christian music artists.

"Working in Smith's favor is that, like [Amy] Grant, he often sells Christian values rather than a specific dogma," wrote Steve Hochman in a March 1993 review of his LA Forum show. "And he does it with enough pop values to blend nicely with secular artists, as well as to give his audience a brand of contemporary pop that they can call their own . . . much of his appeal rests in his vitality and charm.

He has a natural ease onstage and, of course, the hunk appeal that cannot be discounted even in a spiritually oriented context."

Smith's popularity rubbed off on Jars of Clay, who toured with him in 1995, performing their own crossover hit, "Flood." The song was played on CCM, rock, and alternative radio stations, which rarely intersect. "Flood" reached No. 12 on *Billboard*'s Modern Rock Tracks charts, helping to propel its self-titled debut album to double platinum status.

"'Flood' was crazy. We had no idea that it was going to do what it did," said Dan Haseltine, lead vocalist of Jars of Clay. "We were out on tour with Michael W. Smith; we'd play to 20,000 people or 18,000 people in an arena somewhere. Got offstage, get in a van, and drive into any city where we were near and play in some bar for a rock radio station in the same night."

Smith and Jars of Clay weren't the only ones enjoying crossover success.

CCM acts like Bob Carlisle ("Butterfly Kisses"), Kathy Troccoli ("Everything Changes"), Kirk Franklin ("Stomp"), Phillips, Craig & Dean ("Turn Up the Radio"), and Sixpence None the Richer ("Kiss Me") all had big pop hits on the secular charts. In fact, "Kiss Me" was the No. 1 song in the world for 1997. It launched Sixpence None the Richer from New Braunfels, Texas, to international stardom and a spot on *Late Night with David*

"IT WAS SUCH AN EXCITING TIME BECAUSE NOBODY KNEW WHERE THIS WAS GOING TO GO."

Letterman, where Letterman himself appeared to be smitten with lead singer Leigh Nash. Nash had a mad case of the jitters, which the host—and the audience—found endearing.

"The whole experience was amazing. Chris Rock was on that night, and he had gotten on David Letterman's nerves a little bit, and I don't remember why," Nash recalled. "Dave cut that interview a little bit short, and that's the only reason that I was able to have a little bit of time on the couch . . . he was so sweet to me, and I was just so happy that it went well and it hadn't been a disaster. I was a huge Letterman fan, and I kept looking at the band like, *Oh, is this really happening? Holy cow!* It felt like a dream."

CCM artist Steve Taylor, who produced the catchy number, said it was a historical song in many ways. "You could maybe make a case that 'Kiss Me' was perhaps the biggest hit ever to come out of Nashville," he said.

John Styll noted: "Everything just got bigger. More artists. A steady stream of new releases coming out."

The flood of hits meant more money for the labels, which meant artists could get much more creative. And record companies gave them the leeway to do so.

"What happened in the 1990s because of all of that success, the industry had the margin, and margin is where innovation happens in any industry," said John J. Thompson. "When you get profit margin, you get that freedom to experiment."

Freedom to experiment also meant freedom to invest in new talent.

The decade saw a new bumper crop of CCM artists emerge on the scene: DC Talk, Carman, MercyMe, Rebecca St. James, Skillet, Casting Crowns, Switchfoot, 4Him, and Third Day to name just a few.

"There was a huge changing of the guard that happened in the early 1990s in Christian music," said veteran musician Eddie DeGarmo, who later founded his own label, ForeFront Records, and signed DC Talk when no one else would.

Many of these upstart acts got their breaks at the annual Christian Booksellers Association, where thousands gathered in Dallas, Texas, for author signings, seminars, showcase concerts, and the exhibition floor. This was a place where tastemakers minted stars like Steven Curtis Chapman.

STEVEN CURTIS CHAPMAN HAD MULTIPLE HITS IN THE '90s, LIKE "THE GREAT ADVENTURE." HE IS SEEN HERE STRUGGLING TO HOLD HIS MULTIPLE DOVE AWARDS IN 1990.

THE MUSIC GIANTS ALSO EMBRACED JESUS, ALL THE WHILE PUTTING THEIR HANDS IN HIS BACK POCKETS.

"It was such an exciting time because nobody really knew where this was going to go," said Chapman. For the Kentucky native, it meant going all the way. He went on to have one of the most stellar careers in CCM, racking up forty-nine No. 1 radio hits, five Grammys, fifty-nine Dove Awards, and an estimated ten million in album sales.

The combination of established veterans, crossover artists, and emerging acts invigorated CCM to its full earning potential in the 1990s, turning it into a multibillion-dollar industry only two decades after it started.

Word Records did so well that it relocated from its offices in Waco and Irving, Texas, to Nashville to align itself with the reinvigorated and glitzy country music scene. So did Sparrow, who made the move from Chatsworth, California, to Music City, USA. Capitol Records also set up a music division there, as did other majors. Nashville's well-established music scene and plethora of recording studios (not to mention its music-friendly churches) made it a natural place to set up shop. Besides, if a country star suddenly got the urge to record a gospel album, all they had to do was cross the street.

In fact, a few years later, country megastar Alan Jackson did just that, placating his mother's pleas for something from their Baptist church hymnal by recording a two-CD set of old-time gospel hymns called *Precious Memories*. It was precious for both of them: It zoomed to No. 1 on the *Billboard* Contemporary Christian Album charts. Its successor repeated the exercise and was named the Top Christian Album at the *Billboard* Music Awards in 2014.

Dan Haseltine of Jars of Clay said CCM artists not only craved commercial success but also wanted to be innovative in their art. This was their time to shine.

"Our goal was not just to be the Christian version of something else, but it was to own our space in the musical landscape," Haseltine said. "I mean that was the golden age . . . the golden age of Christian music."

It wasn't only the music that was changing. Venues had to change too. The Cornerstone

Festival, an annual Fourth of July Christian music and arts festival outside of Chicago, Illinois, is CCM's Coachella. In 1991, it outgrew its original site and moved to another locale four hours away in Bushnell, Illinois, a farming town of approximately three thousand residents, to accommodate the growing number of attendees. It's a place known for producing dog food, potato chips, rivets, and screws. The new festival site draws close to twenty thousand fans a year who come to hear approximately three hundred musical acts, drink ten-dollar bottles of water, crowd surf, reject religion, and embrace Jesus.

Christian music labels were gobbled up by the majors of the recording industry, so there was more money to throw around, especially when people were willing to spend nearly fifteen dollars on a compact disc that cost less than a buck to produce.

"You see a pretty rapid evolution of how much money there is to spend on artists. So the records start to sound bigger. You see tours getting bigger," said John J. Thompson. "The bands and acts are able to justify spending more money on production. All of this stuff is becoming more competitive with the real world, which all fits into the idea that Christian music is an alternative to something else."

And there were alternatives. CCM became diversified, and every label sold product like never before. Like the secular music scene, the CCM sound splintered. In addition to grunge and alt-rock, there was indie pop, electronic, nu metal, Celtic, country, gospel, worship, and even rap.

The 1990s boom naturally had an impact on radio: K-LOVE, WayFM, Family Life Radio, and Moody Radio expanded the reach of CCM by

JARS OF CLAY, A BAND FROM CENTRAL ILLINOIS, EMERGED ON THE SCENE WITH THEIR CROSSOVER HIT SONG "FLOOD" IN 1995.

NEWSBOYS—FRONTED BY THEN-LEAD-SINGER PETER FURLER—ROCKED ALL AROUND THE WORLD IN THE 1990s, AND CONTINUE TODAY WITH MICHAEL TAIT (FORMERLY DC TALK) AS THE FRONTMAN.

following the corporate format of Clear Channel, which later became iHeartRadio. The medium became more professional and concentrated in the decade, airing in all the major markets. In essence, they were an umbrella brand network that syndicated Christian music to millions of listeners.

There was even a syndicated CCM countdown program like Casey Kasem's "American Top 40" hosted by Jon Rivers. The two-hour, magazine-style show based in Dallas, Texas, counted down the Top 20 Christian music radio songs each week and was broadcast to approximately 1,100 radio stations.

K-LOVE has a particularly interesting history. It originally was started as a single radio station (KCLB-FM) in 1982, in Santa Rosa, California,

by San Francisco disc jockey Bob Anthony, who worked for a station in the Golden Gate City. He bought KCLB out of bankruptcy for $67,000 with the idea of spreading the gospel through the airwaves.

Six years after the station first aired, a nine-thousand-acre brush fire destroyed the main building and the station's main transmitter. Encouraged by public support, the station relocated to the Napa Valley, where a more powerful transmitter was erected. It became K-LOVE in 1988. In the 1990s, K-LOVE expanded its presence by purchasing smaller stations and using satellite technology to expand beyond Northern California. Today, it reaches nearly five million people and carries a signal across much of the United States.

Television followed suit, mostly through the cable networks. By this time the bad blood that had previously existed between televangelists and CCM artists was water under the bridge. The artists went from being the devil's minions to shining stars. In fact, these famous musicians were akin to *Tonight Show* guests and routinely appeared on networks like the Christian Broadcasting Network, The Nashville Network, PTL Television Network, and the Trinity Broadcasting Network. There was no bigger indicator that you were mainstream than being on Pat Robertson's *The 700 Club*. He practically tripped over himself to host CCM stars, whom he treated like Hollywood royalty.

Product also received the star treatment. Albums and compact discs were no longer relegated to Christian bookstores or the back bins of Tower Records, but could now be purchased in big-box chains like Walmart, Target, Best Buy, and Costco. More retail outlets meant more

"SO NOW THE INDUSTRY DESERVES TO BE CALLED THE INDUSTRY."

money for the labels. And that meant attorneys and bean counters ran the show.

The old music executives who had a gambler's mentality, ears for new talent, and a willingness to take risks became dinosaurs overnight. They were replaced in mergers with Ivy Leaguers and CPAs just starting to shave. The men who shaped the industry were given generous buyouts and then were shown the door, and their cigar-reeking offices were fumigated.

The new and young titans placed their bets on established artists, but there was hardly any scratch leftover for developing new talent. The model has been worked to perfection, and it became a template for the entire record industry: Focus on your twenty or thirty biggest earners, cut the rest loose, and count the dollars rolling in. Record executives spent more time fighting over which corner offices, primo parking spots, and company tickets to sporting and cultural events they were entitled to than over label business.

This created a system of haves and have-nots within the recording industry, which was why you saw the same artists being promoted over and over again. It is also why today you see the same faces on the litany of glitzy but meaningless industry award shows—artists like Beyoncé, Taylor Swift, Lady Gaga, J.Lo, and Pitbull.

"When Christian music first started out, it really used to be about artists wanting to reach people through their music," said CCM artist and producer Steve Taylor. "But when money gets

SOME KIND OF ZOMBIE, AUDIO ADRENALINE (1997, FOREFRONT) WAS A CONCEPT ALBUM BASED ON COLOSSIANS 3.

involved, it's really hard to keep that focus. If we lose track of that dichotomy, we're lost."

The days of beach hippies sleeping in bunk beds and garages and playing guitar in the backyard were long gone. Where a dime could not have been found before, CCM was awash in money and cut-throat executives.

"So now the industry deserves to be called the industry, but I'm not sure as it grows into that thing, it's going to retain a lot of its DNA," said John J. Thompson. "It's going to become something else for better or for worse."

It definitely evolved into something else. But whatever the gripes of the day were, these were still the halcyon days of CCM. The artists who emerged as top dogs enjoyed stardom and generously being compensated for their recording work and tours. They even got "mailbox money," otherwise known as royalty checks, when they weren't on the road.

As the industry fired on all cylinders, sales were at an all-time high at nearly $15 billion. Money and cultural influence were off the charts. CCM was a jets and limousine world now.

At the end of the most prosperous decade in CCM history, everyone partied like it was 1999. But as the famous Prince song goes, parties weren't meant to last.

THIRD DAY HAS WON FOUR GRAMMYS AND TWENTY-FIVE DOVE AWARDS AND SOLD AN ESTIMATED SEVEN MILLION ALBUMS SINCE THEIR 1996 DEBUT. THEY PLAYED A FAREWELL TOUR IN 2018.

CHAPTER 10

THAT'S A RAP

All kinds of musical genres have been folded into Contemporary Christian music after a few decades, but one remained on the outside . . . and that was rap.

Rap had been around since the 1970s, evolving at block parties in New York City and mostly staying there until Sugarhill Gang's "Rapper's Delight" (1979) and Blondie's "Rapture" (1980) brought the

Comprised of Toby McKeehan (commonly known as TobyMac), Michael Tait, and Kevin Max, the trio met in 1987 while attending Liberty University in Lynchburg, Virginia. Tait was singing for churches when TobyMac first started rapping. Max came along a little later.

Tait recalled with great clarity that fateful first meeting with TobyMac: "I sang in chapel one day and Toby walked up to me in these black penny

THAT'S A RAP

genre to the fore. But it wasn't until Aerosmith and Run-DMC's 1986 collaboration on "Walk This Way" that things changed forever. The massive hit was the first rap song to be played on both mainstream urban and rock radio.

Rap and hip-hop became part of the popular culture. Everyone began to recognize the signs. Baggy jeans. Oversized shirts. Adidas tennis shoes. Ballcaps, bills parked to the side. Dark shades. And a scowl. To become part of Contemporary Christian music, the genre needed a breakout artist. That was DC Talk.

loafers and these white socks. I was like, 'What do we have here?' He said, 'Hey man, you've got a great voice. Can I buy you a sweet tea from Hardee's?' We started talking, talking, and talking. And we never stopped talking. He was truly my first vanilla best friend in the whole world."

That summer Tait had lined up a slew of summer shows in churches throughout the eastern part of the country. TobyMac needed a summer job and tagged along, running the sound for Tait. According to Tait, his friend did a so-so job. But they were buds, and their bond grew while on the road together. Tait even gave TobyMac an opportunity to sing at the end of each youth service.

"We had this little trick we pulled on the church every Sunday," TobyMac said. "Tait said, 'Yeah, we've got somebody in the back named Toby, but he does something that would be like more for the youth of tomorrow. And the crowd would go, 'What is it?'"

Stallone action flick. Middle America was turned off by the imagery: Uzis and Jacuzzis; baggy pants and dental floss bikinis; drugs and Dom; wads of cash and thumping cars. Many of the rap artists in these videos either went to prison or were shot, which only gave them more street cred in the eyes of their fans.

If the Jesus Movement and heavy metal offended the church in the seventies and eighties, rap

This put the onus on youth ministers who would tell the young men to show everyone what they had. "We'd get up and rap, and the place would become unglued," Tait said. "That's how it all started."

They used this stealth approach because rap had . . . well, a bad rap . . . in white America. The songs, usually seen on *Yo! MTV Raps* glamorized thug life. The genre focused heavily on three things: money, misogyny, and violence. The body counts in some of these videos rivaled a Schwarzenegger or

was its extra-naughty child in the nineties.

By taking this tack, Tait and TobyMac were able to slip their sanitized rap and hip-hop songs into the services. It worked like a charm.

TobyMac and Tait later became a power trio when they heard about Kevin Max, a freshman at Liberty who had an upcoming gig at the university chapel. TobyMac and Tait went to hear him. They looked at each other that night and grinned knowingly, imagining the possibilities that Max could bring to the group.

"We went to see him sing, and man, he could sing. Undoubtedly to this day one of the best singers I've ever heard in my life," TobyMac said. "So after chapel I was like, 'What's up, man?' I shook Kevin's hand and got to meet him a little bit."

TobyMac and Tait didn't mince words or waste Max's time.

"I remember them coming up to me and saying, 'We want you to be in the group,'" Max recalled. "Immediately I was like, 'This isn't going to work.'"

"Here's the deal. This thing on paper shouldn't have worked," Tait said. "Looking at our personalities sometimes, looking at what we were like individually, how we write individually, how we are individually. But at the same time that pull, that tension, made DC Talk great."

They were three alpha males who instinctively sensed that tension was going to be part of the band's equation. Tension kept Aerosmith on top for decades. And there was no love lost within Van Halen. Max was the missing ingredient. He had the killer voice. He had the looks. And he had the X factor.

"I THOUGHT I MADE THIS WHOLE THING UP."

Tait, Max, and TobyMac offered up different talents and influences like rap, rock, and R&B, giving each song its own personality. They were passionate about their art and made sure to communicate honestly about their faith. Whatever doubts they had worked themselves out . . . in the beginning.

TobyMac, who became the group's chief songwriter, was unsure of his writing talents at the start. It was all one steep learning curve, which launched at zero.

"I didn't know Contemporary Christian music existed, so when I wrote my first Christian lyric, I thought I made this whole thing up," TobyMac said.

In time, TobyMac became a very good writer. He hit on topics such as faith, abortion, communication, family dysfunction, and sin and presented them in the earnest way that only youth can.

In late 1988, Eddie DeGarmo recalled that his business partner, Ron Griffin, brought him a demo tape that had been sent to him in the mail by a group calling themselves DC Talk and the One Way Crew. The sound made an impression on him, if only for the reason that all three members were completely different in tone and attitude. The tape didn't particularly scream potential to DeGarmo.

"We were just doing what we loved," TobyMac said. "We weren't trying to market it to anybody. Like, we just loved this kind of music."

A SPIFFED UP DC TALK. ITS MEMBERS INCLUDED KEVIN MAX, TOBYMAC AND MICHAEL TAIT, WHO MET ONE ANOTHER IN COLLEGE.

Max: "When we started getting rejection from labels, it didn't surprise me at all. I was like, 'Nobody's going to get this.'"

But Nashville-based ForeFront Records, for whatever reasons, signed the trio in January 1989. They made the move from Lynchburg to Nashville to display their dedication.

DeGarmo, who was now a partner at ForeFront, gave them their first job in the industry. Part of his new duties was to introduce the label's artists to an audience. DeGarmo & Key took the new groups on tour with them as opening acts, but also put them to work as roadies. Opening up for a band that drew a thousand people a night blew the youngsters' minds.

Their first gig was in 1989 opening for DeGarmo & Key at Wheaton College near Chicago, Illinois. (Wheaton was the alma mater of Billy and Ruth Graham and where they first met.) Little did these three young men know about the hard work of touring.

"They were our roadies for a little while," DeGarmo said. "That didn't last long though because they were so bad at it."

Their enthusiasm didn't exactly match their expertise. They blew out DeGarmo's keyboard with bad wiring, annoyed the veterans with their ineptitude, and often got in the way of everyone. They were ultimately fired from their roadie gig but stayed put as DeGarmo & Key's opening act. They also retained their recording contract.

ForeFront tried to get them radio airtime, but to no avail. Instead, the label gave the band money to make music videos. They scored on their first outing with "Heavenbound," which received heavy rotation on the BET Network despite how two of the band's members were white.

IN JUNE OF 1994, MORE THAN 80,000 PEOPLE SHOWED UP TO HEAR DC TALK AND
MICHAEL W. SMITH PLAY AT A BILLY GRAHAM CRUSADE. THE EVENT WAS A BRIDGE TO
ANOTHER GENERATION FOR THE FAMED EVANGELIST.

The next person to give them an opportunity was a lot bigger than BET.

One night after a show, a person named Rick Marshall, director of Crusades/Missions for the Billy Graham Evangelistic Association, pulled them aside after a concert and said, "I'd like for you to play a show. We're changing what Billy Graham has been." The famed evangelist decided that his organization was going to reach the next generation by changing the program and organizing a rock concert for youth.

"I went to Billy in the fall of '93 and said, 'Would you give us permission to do an experiment?'" Marshall said. The idea was to surround Graham's message with youthful dressing that would ultimately expose the younger audience to God's word.

"Music is the popular expression of their culture," said Marshall, a father of four. "If you don't have the music, you don't have the kids . . . the idea

IT WAS FELT THAT GRAHAM WAS MAKING THE WRONG DECISION.

of a concert is a much more contemporary image for kids rather than the concept of a crusade."

Marshall also told his then seventy-five-year-old boss that his message would not get lost in the music. "I told him the youth need straight talk from a caring adult," Marshall recalled. "I said, 'Mr. Graham, that's you.'"

It was a brilliant concept, but Michael Tait was concerned this might not be a good fit.

"Okay, they do know what we do, right?" Tait said. "I said to myself, 'We're going to come in as young cats, bouncing all over the stage, sweatpants on, hats turned sideways.'"

Within the Graham organization, the idea was met with lots of opposition. It was felt that Graham was making the wrong decision.

The famed evangelist turned to his board for answers.

Greg Laurie was the youngest board member of the Billy Graham Evangelistic Association at the time this decision took place. He thought it was a deft move on Graham's part.

"Billy was always ahead of the curve on things like this, but to do it in his seventies was surprising and refreshing," Laurie said. "Not all of my fellow board members supported this idea, but I did."

Shortly after Graham decided to move ahead with his decision, he invited the group to his home. TobyMac remembers walking into his house in Montreat, North Carolina, heart racing.

"We are so grateful to be here," TobyMac told Ruth Graham. "We're going to walk out into a stadium and play the music that we love."

The first lady of evangelism told the young man the pleasure was all hers.

"Ruth Graham said, 'What do you mean, Toby? We know what this is . . . DC Talk stocks the pond so that Billy can do some fishing,'" TobyMac laughed when recalling that conversation.

Later the group learned that Graham's organization didn't want to freak out the legendary evangelist, so they put him in a separate room with a TV monitor to watch DC Talk onstage. But the volume was turned down.

June 1994. Cleveland Coliseum. Eighty thousand people showed up to hear DC Talk and Michael W. Smith play at a Billy Graham Crusade Youth Night.

"I remember showing up and thinking, 'Wow, we are making history,'" said Michael W. Smith. "Me and DC Talk at a Billy Graham Crusade. I mean, it is full-on. And then all of a sudden Billy walks to the podium and the place just explodes. Billy gave one of the most compelling sermons I've ever heard him do."

Graham read the lyrics to a DC Talk song called "The Hard Way" as part of his message. The song is about a stubborn sinner who seeks redemption time and time again and has to learn his lessons "the hard way" because he has failed to yield to the Lord. TobyMac had just finished the song,

THEIR SUCCESS OPENED THE DOOR FOR OTHER MAINSTREAM RAP, HIP-HOP, AND R&B ARTISTS.

and Graham's sermon absolutely tore him apart. He started crying, as did the others in the group.

"Man, every memory in my life flashed back," Michael Tait said. "I'm walking onstage right now with Billy Graham who I saw as a kid. It was overwhelming."

Greg Laurie was there that night as well and remembers rapturous applause for DC Talk and Michael W. Smith. However, the audience saved the best for last.

"Billy received a resounding ovation from the young people that night, even greater than the bands," Laurie recalled. "When Billy traveled overseas, he sometimes needed translators so he could be heard in the language of the people he was addressing. These bands were Billy's bridge to a new generation, interpreters of sorts. The results spoke volumes."

As Ruth Graham predicted, her husband caught a lot of fish that night. After Billy delivered his sermon, thousands of Cleveland-area folks flocked to the field to be near the podium where Billy stood, where they dedicated their lives to Christ.

"We ran out of counselors. We ran out of literature," Marshall recalled. "You could not see a blade of grass in the stadium."

Cleveland was a milestone for everyone involved, especially DC Talk, because the group had been validated by Billy Graham.

"Outside of this church thing, I think I could argue that he [Graham] turned the page for all of us when it comes to music and how we can express ourselves in the arts," TobyMac said. "We don't have to do it the way it was done before. We can do it the way we want to do it. And Billy Graham said, 'That's valuable.'"

And they were valuable. Not only had they become the most successful rap group in CCM, but arguably the most successful band in all of the 1990s.

"Nobody was doing what DC Talk was doing," said Michael W. Smith. "They were the perfect storm. They just tapped into something."

John Styll initially saw them as a passing fad but realized the band and the genre had staying power. "Frankly, I'm surprised by it all. I thought it [rap] was really a trendy, faddish sort of thing when it first started," Styll said. "But suddenly we've got rap albums on our Christian-rock chart."

Their success opened the door for other mainstream rap, hip-hop, and R&B artists such as Lecrae, NF, Andy Mineo, Wande, nobigdyl, and Social Club Misfits.

LECRAE IS A HIP-HOP ARTIST, SONGWRITER, RECORDING ARTIST, ACTOR, AUTHOR AND ENTREPRENEUR. IN 2013 HE BECAME THE FIRST HIP-HOP ARTIST TO WIN A GRAMMY FOR BEST GOSPEL ALBUM (*GRAVITY*).

However, none were as big as DC Talk. They were like a supernova that engulfed Mother Earth. In addition to tons of swagger, they had catchy songs, platinum albums, groundbreaking videos, sold-out concerts . . . the works.

They were making good money. Great money. Oh-my-gracious money. Kevin Max even cut his lawn in two-thousand-dollar Ralph Lauren suede pants.

"I said, 'Kevin, what in the world are you doing?'" Michael Tait recalled. It was a sign they were becoming true stars.

But the higher the climb, the harder the fall. The *Washington Post* thought these young Christians were crass and condescending. They wrote in one review: "DC Talk takes the idea of

JESUS FREAK (1995, FOREFRONT) DC TALK'S FOURTH STUDIO ALBUM, IS CONSIDERED A SEMINAL WORK, WHICH INCORPORATES ELEMENTS OF GRUNGE AND HARD ROCK.

putting the Gospel into the vernacular to ridiculous lengths with its sacred hip-hop. Introducing itself as 'two honkies and a Negro serving the Lord,' the young trio—backed by three musicians and four energetic dancers—seemed like Up with People directed by Marky Mark."

Oddly enough, similar thoughts were going through the minds of the band. Mentally, their cohesion was beginning to crack with the mounting success. They bickered, pulled power plays, and sometimes even brawled.

"One time, Mike and I got into a really big argument on the tour bus, and we were yelling and pushing each other so much that the bus was going back and forth, rocking," Max recalled. "The show would start, and I wouldn't come on stage. They would be rolling into the second song, and I would finally be like, 'Okay, I need to go out there.'"

Musician Will Turpin knows what it's like to be under that intense spotlight. As bassist and cofounding member of Collective Soul, his group also experienced rapid stardom in the 1990s. They even performed a couple of festivals with DC Talk. Turpin said fame doesn't come with a handbook, and while no one can properly prepare for it, everyone has to rise to the occasion.

"Fame simply boils down to more work and more responsibility, and everybody has to know their lane," Turpin said. "When a group becomes successful, it's now a partnership, and you must know or understand what your role is. If the roles aren't defined, there's going to be trouble."

Turpin said touring can exacerbate personality conflicts and tear a band apart. "You're stuck with the same people over long periods of time, and it can get intense," Turpin said. "Some artists just can't handle that because they're not made for the road."

THEY QUICKLY BEGAN SPLINTERING UNDER THE WEIGHT OF SUCCESS.

This combustibility in a group dynamic was not uncommon, especially on tour. Groups like the Who, Aerosmith, Van Halen, the Police, and Oasis thrived on this negative energy and organized chaos and somehow were able to funnel it into the music. But that kind of alchemy can only last for so long.

"Yeah, there was tension," said Audio Adrenaline's Mark Stuart, who toured with DC Talk. "Those guys were held together with duct tape and prayer."

They quickly began splintering under the weight of success. At one point, they couldn't stand to even look at or speak to each other.

TobyMac recalled a time on the *Supernatural* tour when he had a runner take him to a local Barnes & Noble where he wanted to grab a cup of coffee, chill, and read a book or paper to unwind. He was in a van on the passenger side, and as the driver pulled up to the store, he noticed Kevin sitting inside the café drinking coffee. For whatever reasons, TobyMac didn't want to converse that day with Kevin and asked the driver to take him to another Barnes & Noble in the area. He had never done anything like that before. He didn't want any fireworks before the show and purposely avoided any confrontation. When they drove away, TobyMac felt it was time to take a break from the group.

They did take a break, but after two decades, it appears to be a permanent one.

"I don't look at it as regret that we went our separate ways in 2000," Kevin Max said. "I think the timing was right. I've had a magnificent life. It was a huge learning curve for me, and I feel like what's informed me as an artist more than anything is to see ultimate success and ultimate failure and to live in the valley of that."

DC Talk broke up at the start of the millennium. Tait went on to become the lead singer for the Newsboys, a hugely successful CCM band. Max had a brief stint as lead singer for Audio Adrenaline but focused more on writing poetry and performing as a solo artist, mostly in smaller venues. And TobyMac went on to superstardom, just as Justin Timberlake did when he left NSYNC.

In a way, DC Talk is in the same enviable position as the Beatles and Oasis; decades after their breakup, fans are still yearning for a reunion. Their fame was built on a

KIRK FRANKLIN IS THE BIGGEST GOSPEL STAR IN CONTEMPORARY CHRISTIAN MUSIC TODAY. IN THE 1990S, HE WAS UNSTOPPABLE.

vision of marrying two genres. But another artist was coming along who would do the same thing and become even bigger by melding CCM, gospel, and rap.

His name was Kirk Franklin.

"There's no question that Kirk Franklin is the biggest gospel music artist of our time," said Bill Reeves, CEO of K-LOVE.

Arguably, he's the biggest gospel music artist of *all* time. But his success story has a sad beginning. He was given up for adoption by his parents.

Franklin recalled: "I remember the hole in my soul as a little kid. I realized I was adopted when my mother made the decision when she didn't want to be a mother. I think I was about two or three. And the lady who adopted me—her name was Gertrude—she biologically was my great, great, great aunt. She was born not being able to vote and not being able to drink where other people could drink or walk where other people could walk. I remember her singing hymns in the house. Right in the front of the house there was a piano . . . I still have that piano. There was something very romantic between me and that piano as a kid, but it was always ideas about songs about Jesus. There was something about music even at an early age [and] about the idea of God because, as a kid, that's all that it is. The idea of God pulled at a very early age in my heart."

He sang with church choirs and played piano. His aunt collected aluminum cans to pay for his lessons. Had she not, the gospel world would be much different.

Despite writing songs for the church, he was very much a hip-hop kid. He knew there was something going on between him and songwriting. He knew people liked his music, and he knew they liked him. The latter part—love and acceptance—was what especially drove him.

There wasn't much love at the start of Franklin's career. He couldn't get a record deal. He couldn't get signed. He couldn't get anything.

The music wasn't very good, he was told. The songwriting wasn't good enough either. He got discouraged and was down-and-out for a little while.

"I was a couple of months behind on my rent, and I finally did get evicted because I was so late so many times that I had to move out at night because I didn't want anyone to know I was getting kicked out," Franklin said.

But a break finally came along. He played an event where the guest artist was Daryl Coley. Coley's wife had a distribution deal with a record company

THERE WASN'T MUCH LOVE AT THE START OF FRANKLIN'S CAREER.

who signed him for $7,000. It was the foot in the door that he needed.

In the 1990s Franklin was unstoppable. He came out with "Stomp," a mainstream hit in 1995. People heard it often on *The Tonight Show*. He was inventing his own genre, and it was immediately recognized.

"They played 'Stomp' in the club," said comedian Bone Hampton. "I was watching people dancing to 'Stomp' in the way that I know you ain't supposed to be dancing in the club. I was like, 'You can't be dancing this way to this song!'"

"Stomp" became big in the Christian community because it became big in pop culture. "Some people think of that as a moment when CCM got a little more integrated," said John J. Thompson. "You're too late to the party to claim that you had anything to do with 'Stomp.' I'm sorry, CCM. That's not your song. That's Kirk Franklin going to the mainstream and you guys playing catch-up."

The song caused an uprising in the church.

"It was a problem," Franklin recalled. "There

"THERE WAS SO MUCH DRAMA IN THE CHURCH."

was so much drama in the church, man, and there was a lot of negative feedback."

Church groups soon showed up to protest at his concerts, telling him that he was going to hell and needed to repent because his moves were of the devil. Franklin was a bridge builder and approached a bearded, twentysomething protester sporting a ballcap and using a bullhorn. Franklin asked him if he'd be willing to open up the Bible to review exactly what sin he was committing. Then he stuck out his hand to shake on it.

"I'm not going to shake your hand, sir," the protestor replied.

When "Stomp" was climbing high on the charts, Franklin was at a church conference where close to sixty thousand people were in attendance. A couple of church pastors who were friends met him in the lobby. They told him another pastor there at the conference had spoken out against him. Franklin went upstairs to his hotel room and sat on the bathroom floor. He was seething.

"God, man . . . God, I didn't ask for this. I didn't ask to be criticized. I just want to be liked," Franklin said to himself. He later recalled of that moment: "I just remember being very upset at God, and the Lord spoke to my heart: 'If they don't have no prints on their hands, no scars on their forehead, you owe them no explanation.'"

This incident made him take stock of his life. Franklin now knows that what he does is not what he is.

"When it comes to my value, when it comes to the little boy that just wanted to be liked by his mom and his daddy, I'm better than I was," Franklin said. "I still have a lot of growing to do. I still have moments where I fall back into it. And for somebody that's been an addict of needing the approval and praise of people, that has added a layer of my journey."

His journey continues. Franklin is still performing and is at the top of his game.

"Kirk has been an amazing presence as an artist, as a songwriter, as a producer," said John J. Thompson. "I'm not sure that we deserve him, but I'm glad as an artist that he hasn't given up on us."

The CCM universe was now complete. There was country, metal, gospel, rap, pop, alt-rock, and hip-hop. Like DC Talk at Billy Graham's Crusade, the genre had penetrated all levels of the church and music industry. What could possibly go wrong?

A lot, it turned out.

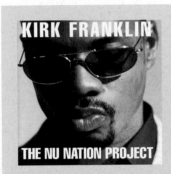

THE NU NATION PROJECT, (1998, GOSPOCENTRIC), CONTAINED "STOMP," THE DANCE CLUB HIT AND 1995 SINGLE.

KIRK FRANKLIN PERFORMING AT THE 2015 DOVE AWARDS.

MINER SHAK

CHAPTER 11

AFTER THE
GOLD RUSH

The beginning of the end commenced in 1998 in Cape Cod, Massachusetts. A seventeen-year-old named Shawn Fanning was in his bedroom listening to music on his headphones with a jack plugged into his computer. He was doing his two favorite things at once: programming and rocking out to his favorite band, Metallica.

He was new to the area. After being bounced around in the foster care system, he was back with his family after being away for a period.

Fanning was an awkward kid who felt out of place because he was usually the newcomer wherever he went. Basketball was a quick way to forge friendships. Like all new kids on the blacktop, he got teased. They especially ragged on his short, frizzy hair. On the court, he was called "Nappy." Later, when he gained acceptance, it was changed to "Napster," which later became his handle online in hacking chat rooms.

The teen's nickname carried over to college, when he attended Boston's Northeastern University and majored in computer science. When he wasn't studying, playing basketball, or partying with friends, Fanning developed software inside his tiny dorm room in Kennedy Hall, which he named Napster. Late into his first quarter, he was helping out a roommate with a problem he was having downloading MP3 files from a search engine. He did this by writing code, which he deemed "a small project." He began sharing these files—which were free—with others. It turned out to be a big hit with his friends. Demand spread, and so did his energy to work on his experiment.

Fanning spent so much time working out the bugs in his software that it compromised his schoolwork and time for socializing. He became so engrossed in the Napster concept that he left the university. It wasn't a foolish decision. Fanning knew he was onto something.

AFTER THE
GOLD RUSH

His software linked computers and allowed users to access each other's MP3 audio files, creating a service that made music available instantaneously and free. And for those who still preferred CDs, users could burn multiple copies for all their friends.

"It was something that provided a better, more reliable, and fun way for people to share music and see each other's music collection," Fanning told the BBC World Service. "For the first time, this full

"All the way back in the eighties, when music got turned back into zeros and ones, you had the inevitability created by digitization," said John J. Thompson. "But it was only a question of time between compression of file sizes and expansion of file transfer capability over data wires. And when those two things eventually cross and you're able to transmit music conveniently, the era of people spending fifteen-dollars-plus to buy a full CD is over."

history of recorded music was available online to everyone instantly."

With the help of his friend and budding entrepreneur Sean Parker (who was also involved with the evolution of Facebook), Fanning launched Napster in June 1999. The service didn't just "disrupt" the recording industry with this form of mass piracy; it collapsed it, burning it to the ground.

Four months after Napster was founded, approximately 150,000 people had signed up. A year later it had 26.4 million verified users.

Up to that point, consumers were willing to make a special trip to the record store to spend their money on a CD that had a couple of songs they liked. With Napster, they didn't even have to waste their time or gas. They could get their music sitting in their pajamas, munching on saltines and eating Cheez Whiz from the can. And the price was right: free.

This was a paradigm shift for both executives and artists. The music industry shifted from an album-oriented medium to a playlist and

THE ARRIVAL OF NAPSTER AND SEVERAL OTHER MUSIC SERVICES IN THE LATE 1990S MEANT THE DIGITAL REVOLUTION WAS AT HAND, WHICH CHANGED THE WAY PEOPLE CONSUMED MUSIC.

singles-based model. Sadly, the music was nearly mortally wounded. The album as an art form in itself—a series of linked songs that created something greater than the sum of its parts—almost disappeared. There would be no more masterpieces or concept albums like *The Dark Side of the Moon* by Pink Floyd, *Exile on Main Street* by the Rolling Stones, *Hotel California* by the Eagles, *Déjà vu* by Crosby, Stills, Nash & Young, or *Sgt. Pepper's Lonely Hearts Club Band* by the Beatles.

Record industry executives were initially slow in their response to this new disruptor, even though they definitely knew about it. They held meetings in exotic locales like London, Tokyo, Maui, and Florence to discuss the matter, but it was mainly to pat each other on the back and talk about how wonderful they were. They schmoozed, drank booze, smoked cigars, and considered themselves untouchable as they lounged in their poolside suites and villas. Foolishly.

"In the late '90s, my staff started monitoring the online space, and we really did see a significant amount of interest in MP3 all of a sudden because of its ability to compress a music file," said Hilary Rosen, who headed up the Recording Industry Association of America (RIAA), the trade organization that represents the US recording industry. "I think there really wasn't any sort of panic in the industry in the early days. My team did look at it and saw it as not really as much of a threat as an opportunity."

But that changed as Napster gained a robust following. When the record industry noticed sales slipping and Napster's eighty million registered users, it finally got their attention.

Rosen called for an emergency board meeting at the Four Seasons Hotel in Los Angeles on February 24, 2000, the night after the Grammy Awards. The news she had to deliver to these titans wasn't good. In fact, it was downright grim.

"You know about Napster," she started. "We've already sued them, and we're going to win, but it's going to take a while. In the meantime, the media has been all over Napster and that's just making it more popular by the hour. You need to understand how bad this is."

Rosen nodded her head to a staff member who duly flipped open a laptop, downloaded the Napster software application, and registered for the service. This task was accomplished in a matter of seconds, not minutes. Once fully registered, she called on board members to request a few song titles.

"Livin' La Vida Loca" was the first title shouted back—the Ricky Martin song that started the Latin pop explosion of the late nineties and made the swivel-hipped singer a household name. The tune came up instantly on Napster.

Rosen asked for another title. Someone suggested "Baby One More Time" by Britney Spears. Check. Napster had that too. Board members started looking at each other, loosening their collars and scanning the room.

Rosen suggested those were way too easy. How about something a little more obscure or recent? "Bye Bye Bye" by NSYNC was suggested. The song had only been playing on the radio for a few days. It was so new, in fact, that the CD hadn't even seen the light of day. Yep, Rosen's assistant showed that Napster offered that too.

A hush fell over the room. Rosen remained silent, letting these record chiefs take in the seriousness of this situation.

"Millions are listening to music this way," she said, adding that the service Napster provided was free. One executive deadpanned that free was a compelling price point and was going to be hard to beat.

Except it wasn't free for the record moguls. This was costing them billions. In 2000 alone, total recording sales decreased by 33 percent.

The five largest record labels—Sony, Warner, BMG, EMI, and Universal—along with a couple of artists (Metallica and Dr. Dre) launched lawsuits against Napster and several other music services (Gnutella, LimeWire, Kazaa, and Grokster) in federal court, claiming copyright infringement. They did it to stem the tide of the digital threat, claiming this new technology would rob them of billions in profits. So they sued not only these music services but more than fifteen thousand consumers to teach them a lesson for downloading free music. Their actions created the opposite effect, and a backlash arose among fans who felt the industry had taken advantage of artists and gouged customers for far too long. Or as one twenty-one-year-old college

THIS WAS COSTING THEM BILLIONS.

student told a *Charlotte Observer* reporter, "I know it's illegal. But who am I to stand in the way of karma kicking the music industry's [tail]?"

John Styll recalled: "There were lawsuits everywhere trying to get rid of Napster, LimeWire, and all of these different things popping up. It was like Whac-A-Mole because they were trying to knock them out because people were stealing music. That's how they saw it—stealing music. And Christian music was not immune."

The record labels spent years in court and millions in legal bills. Napster was felled by attorney's fees and eventually filed for bankruptcy. Its assets were liquidated, and its naming rights were snapped up by another user. By the time it was all said and done, Steve Jobs had created a cost-effective service called iTunes, catching everyone by surprise.

The digital revolution was at hand, which meant the "rockonomics" could no longer work under the new system. Record label giants drastically cut their staff and artist rosters. They also moved out of their expensive office digs into more affordable spaces. Image went out the window. The smaller labels folded, declared bankruptcy, or were bought out. Out of this new model evolved the 360-deal, where labels now get an entire piece of the artist pie, including merchandising and touring revenue.

The impact was felt harder initially on the secular side, which pushed many established artists to go the indie route. That meant setting up their own shop without roster support, producing and distributing their own albums, and making and paying for all of their own artistic choices, including photo and video shoots, sound engineers, road crew, etc. But they also reaped the financial benefits by keeping more of the profit in their own pockets. Collective Soul, who was signed to Atlantic Records, was one of the first major bands to successfully pull this off once their contract expired in 2001.

"We can sell more records and make even more money. Look, Atlantic paid $6.5 million rent for its company headquarters. The Atlantic artists paid that bill. How's that fair?" said Collective Soul lead singer, Ed Roland. "We still have a lot of friends at Atlantic, and there are some really great people there. We love them. It's corporate America, that's the problem. The record industry is a beast that can't control itself."

Roland said there were pros and cons to the group's bold move, but mostly pros. "We're having to hustle more, since we don't have very deep pockets. You have to be more clever, but it's great to know that everything we do is coming back to our world. With a major label, there's obvious pros and cons, but you never know where their agenda lies."

Somehow, it was thought that the Contemporary Christian genre would not succumb to the same threats. The fans were different. They were Christians, for heaven's sake. They didn't steal, right?

That turned out not to be the case. Original sin and all.

"WE'RE HAVING TO HUSTLE MORE, SINCE WE DON'T HAVE VERY DEEP POCKETS."

Still, it took a bit more time. Christian music sales were still heavenly in 2001. In fact, it had its best sales that year while overall sales declined by 2.8 percent. CCM artists sold almost fifty million albums that year, up 12 percent from 2000 according to SoundScan, the service that tracked album and CD sales.

The secular labels were still producing Christian music, but it was a tower they didn't see surrounded by an army. They would see it clearly in time.

By March 2003, the narrative dramatically shifted. That's when Apple opened its iTunes Store with a catalog of two hundred thousand songs for just ninety-nine cents apiece. They decimated the competition.

"It's as if someone rode up Mount Everest and just flew off the other side," said John J. Thompson.

"Statistically, the sales losses due to file sharing was exactly the same in the Christian world as it was to the mainstream music world," said John Styll. "We could not convince the Christian audience that it was stealing, that it was wrong. Free music is free music, and it's irresistible. When people started sharing files, sales plummeted."

The secular and Christian record labels weren't the only ones impacted; record stores went the way of the buggy whip and dodo bird, fading into the sunset. Retail space and sections for music and CDs shrank exponentially. Eventually, Christian bookstores also went extinct.

"There were a lot of people who'd felt as if we'd lost our way with all of that celebrity. There seemed to be a lot of ego," said Michael W. Smith. "There seemed to be a lot of who's No. 1? Who's selling the most records? I think we'd lost our way. I think we need something to help us refocus."

A reckoning was at hand, but no one really knew it at the time.

Contemporary Christian music and rock artist John Elefante started his producing career

CECE WINANS (2001, WELLSPRING GOSPEL/SPARROW RECORDS), IS THE SELF-TITLED ALBUM BY THE GRAMMY AND DOVE-WINNING GOSPEL SINGER FROM DETROIT.

in the 1980s. In 1993, he and his brother, Dino, plunked down $90,000 on a two-acre lot and broke ground that same year on a 28,000-square-foot studio in Franklin, Tennessee, called Sound Kitchen. The Elefante brothers planned on renting space to other artists as well as using the top-shelf facilities for their own productions, including recording as Mastedon, their popular Christian metal band.

Each recording studio came with its own private lounge. Sound Kitchen also featured a cozy dining room and full-blown kitchen where Elefante's parents cooked tasty Italian meals for the artists. Autographed plates by the artists hung on the walls. Its location was also ideal because many recording artists lived in the area and often commuted in bumper-to-bumper traffic to Music Row in downtown Nashville. They no longer wanted to record there once they got a taste of Sound Kitchen.

"It was in the Cool Springs neighborhood, which had all of these great new stores and restaurants. We had an eight-to-ten-year run where you couldn't even get a room. We were booked that far in advance," Elefante said. "Every Friday we'd bring in a hot dog cart—the dirty water dogs from New York City—into the courtyard. I remember one Friday we had a lot of major music stars and producers in the studio, and we took a break to hang out and eat hot dogs. Dino and I would look at each other and not say a word. I mean, we were a couple of knuckleheads from California, and all of these big names are recording in our studio. But we

knew what the other was thinking: 'Man, this place is sooo happening.'"

Indeed, it was. Sound Kitchen's business was so good that it expanded three years after it initially opened, totaling eighty thousand square feet, making it the Southeast's largest recording facility.

Artists such as Bruce Springsteen, Dolly Parton, Julio Iglesias, Brooks & Dunn, Faith Hill, Tim McGraw, Michael W. Smith, Alan Jackson, Bon Jovi, Buddy Guy, and Petra all recorded there, hung out with each other, shared pasta and meatballs with the Elefantes, or chowed on New York–style hot dogs on Fridays.

Fast forward to 2003. John Elefante began noticing a disturbing trend in the new millennium: Sound Kitchen numbers were heading in a slow but steady downward spiral. He gathered his staff and told them in a meeting that the numbers no longer made sense, and he and his brother had to get out while they could. The Elefantes sold the facility that year to Texas-based Weston Entertainment for an undisclosed sum. The new owners were gracious enough to keep the staff intact.

Artists also had to change the way they did business. In this new era, they were forced to be nimble, adaptable, and fan-friendly. According to Randy Stonehill, they also had to be faithful.

"The funny thing to me is that still, in all, being with a record company, though it had its advantages, it was like working for the bank," said Stonehill, who had been with Word Records for

FAMED GUITARISTS PHIL KEAGGY AND RANDY STONEHILL WERE PART OF THE EARLY YEARS OF JESUS MUSIC, AND WITNESSED ITS GROWING PAINS THROUGH INCREDIBLY PROSPEROUS YEARS AND INTO THE INDUSTRY'S MOST DIFFICULT DAYS OF THE DIGITAL REVOLUTION.

"Record companies are, for the most part these days . . . almost obsolete," Stonehill said. "And the smaller part of me just had to snicker a little bit and say, 'Aw, you guys . . . you always thought that you were going to have everyone over a barrel.' Now it is a very interesting time again because, again, the Lord is faithful. Creativity belongs to Him."

Creativity belongs to the Lord, but it's channeled through the artist. That's why it's called the "divine spark." And that spark got a boost from technology.

With Pro Tools and the emergence of home studios, analog gave way to digital. Recording technology became more compact and inexpensive. Artists were mostly recording their new material on the cheap and in a matter of days and weeks, not for months in an expensive studio. And even if they still had their old distribution pipeline, artists who sold millions had to come back down to planet Earth. Egos crashed because the market coldly informed them they weren't as hot as once before.

With royalty checks drying up, artists now had to rely on constant touring to fill in the revenue gaps. That meant spending a minimum of 60 to 70

close to twenty years before they dropped him from their roster. "It was a strange feeling, but it was also a good feeling because I thought, *Now, wait a minute. I've been practicing, and I'm pretty good. I have a sense of calling here. I don't have to rely on a record company. I need to rely on God.*"

Stonehill also felt the major record labels had no one else to blame but themselves for the industry imploding.

CREATIVITY BELONGS TO THE LORD, BUT IT'S CHANNELED THROUGH THE ARTIST.

percent of their time on the road and not necessarily promoting new product. They toured to keep their name in circulation and to prevent fading from the public spotlight. In addition to the usual venues, artists now played more fan-friendly gigs such as festivals, cruise ships, wineries, and sporting events. VIP meet and greets also became de rigueur and another source of artist revenue.

With the constant touring, introducing new material was mostly a thing of the past. Many acts had to shape up their nightly playlists to resemble a greatest-hits show, which eliminated a lot of the artistry for many of them. But they either played or stayed home . . . and starved.

And when they were at home, they posted on Facebook and other social media to personally interact with fans, play advance tracks, host promotional giveaways and autographs, and post old photos or new video snippets of their everyday lives in order to "build community."

This was the new reality of the business.

"Get hot or go home" was no longer the slogan of the industry. It was now "stayin' alive." The rock gods had been cast out of heaven, never to return.

MUSICIANS AND ARTISTS TODAY OFTEN UTILIZE THE CONVENIENCE OF HOME STUDIOS TO CREATE NEW MUSIC, THANKS TO THE DIGITAL REVOLUTION.

CHAPTER 12

FOR SUCH A
TIME AS THIS

t was March 2, 2001, at 2:58 a.m. Michael W. Smith suddenly woke up. In the darkness, he heard a voice say, "For such a time as this."

Not many words, and those few were open to interpretation. But it was clear as an Old Testament revelation that God was giving him a directive: Make a worship album.

Smith had been a worship leader for twenty years and had written worship songs, but they never

"I'm not going to do it," he defiantly told God.

He blew it off. A week or two later, he woke up again in the middle of the night. He was practically jolted. This time God wasn't so quiet. Neither was God quiet when he called the young Samuel three times. Samuel kept thinking it was the high priest, Eli, calling him in the night, but it was the Lord God himself who was calling out to the young man.

FOR SUCH A
TIME AS THIS

appeared on any of his albums. It was an audacious thought because Smith had built his career on Christian pop and was heavily influenced by the Beatles and Elton John. He didn't think it was a good fit with his music career.

"I didn't want to make a worship record," Smith said. "I mean, I was this pop artist, and I was afraid of what everybody would think. I was afraid it would fail."

Smith was reluctant to break ranks now despite such clearly defined marching orders and nothing to misinterpret. He made up his mind.

Samuel and Michael W. Smith had to learn what the voice of the Lord God sounded like.

"I heard this audible voice say, 'For such a time as this,'" Smith recalled. "I just wrestled with it, and I blew it off, and three weeks later I heard it again. Really, really loud voice. 'For such a time as this.'"

This statement—"for such a time as this"—is from the Old Testament book of Esther. She was a beautiful Jewish maiden who became the queen of Persia after being married to the powerful and feared king, Artaxerxes.

A wicked man named Haman wanted to have all the Jewish people rounded up and killed as part of a vendetta he had against a Jew he hated named Mordecai. Haman even got the unwitting king of Persia to sign the decree. Queen Esther was completely oblivious to what was happening to her people, but her Uncle Mordecai made her aware when he wrote a letter to her, reminding her she was a Jew who would not be spared from this slaugh-

tension into the story, leaving us with her giving one of the most memorable quotes from the Old Testament: "If I perish, I perish" (Esther 4:16 NIV).

Like Esther, Smith understood he could use his influence to change the outcome of many people. After a while, he knew it was useless to argue with his Maker and finally relented. Besides, he suspected he wouldn't get any sleep until he did it. He really had no choice.

ter. Then Mordecai asked whether Esther had not indeed been set in a place of influence in the palace with access to the king for a reason, writing, "And who knows but that you have come to your royal position for such a time as this?" (Esther 4:14 NIV).

The potential penalty for approaching the king without invitation in those days was punishment by death regardless of who you were; this even applied to the queen. Esther made the decision to do so on behalf of her people, knowing the possible and dire consequence. Her brave choice brings a great dynamic and

"Okay, I'm gonna do it," Smith told God. "I'm gonna make this first worship album."

God, in his wisdom, taught Samuel to recognize his voice. In his sovereignty, God used Esther to thwart the eradication of the Jews. And in his love for his people of the twenty-first century, he gave Smith the opportunity to respond to the challenge of drawing hearts to God through his music.

Smith would call the album *Worship*, and a concept soon began to take shape. Smith wanted songs on this new album to "say what I would want to say in a prayer song to God." He envisioned a mix of traditional and modern-day hymns. It was an eclectic collection, combining songs like U2's "40" (Smith and Bono enjoyed a nice friendship); Rich Mullins's "Awesome God"; a ballad composition called "Above All" (which he sang at George W. Bush's inaugural prayer service); and "Forever," a touching song by budding artist Chris Tomlin.

Part of the concept was an all-star choir of CCM artists and musicians recording an entire album of worship songs in front of a live audience. There were about sixty artists he had in mind—a choir, bands, instrumentalists, and vocalists. Some of those he enlisted included Amy Grant, Darwin Hobbs, Chris Rice, Mark Schultz, Shaun Groves, Greg Long, Cindy Morgan, Ginny Owens, Out of Eden, members of Plus One, and the trio of Phillips, Craig & Dean.

It sounded simple enough, but there was a question of ego and logistics. The situation was not unlike producer Quincy Jones's session for "We Are the World," where he gathered the Who's Who of rock and pop stars the night of the 1985 Grammys and got them to record the charity single in an all-night marathon session. Even though these CCM stars weren't as world famous as Michael Jackson, Tina Turner, or Stevie Wonder, Smith still worried. They were, after all, the top artists of their genre.

IT WAS AN INSPIRED COMMUNAL EXPERIENCE AND EVERY MINUTE WAS DIVINELY CONSCRIPTED.

"I said, 'I want every artist who will do it to check their egos at the door and come and be in the choir,'" Smith recalled.

He chartered the artists on three separate planes in June to take them to Lakeland, Florida, where they would perform in front of a standing-room-only crowd of nine thousand people in the cavernous Carpenter's Home Church.

The concert wasn't an evening of furthering anyone's careers, but one of worship. And it sounded like nothing before. This music had electric and acoustic guitars, bass, percussion, keyboards, and an orchestra, all playing and singing in unison.

LEADING THE CHARGE ON *WORSHIP* WAS LIKE RIDING A WILD STALLION, RECALLED MICHAEL W. SMITH. HE SAID: "ABOUT HALFWAY THROUGH IT, I WAS JUST HANGING ON; I WAS LIKE NOT IN CHARGE. I LITERALLY DON'T HAVE THE REINS IN MY HANDS." *WORSHIP* RECEIVED A 2002 DOVE AWARD FOR BEST PRAISE AND WORSHIP ALBUM OF THE YEAR, AND "ABOVE ALL" WON INSPIRATIONAL SONG OF THE YEAR.

Smith likened it to riding a wild stallion.

"About halfway through it, I was just hanging on; I was like not in charge," said Smith, who led the group of recording veterans at the piano. "I literally don't have the reins in my hand. I do not have the reins in my hand," he repeated.

From the first bar of music (Tomlin's "Forever"), all nine thousand were on their feet, singing and clapping in unison.

There were no solos, and several of the evening's highlights occurred when no lyrics were being sung. It was an inspired communal experience, and every minute was divinely conscripted.

"The recording of that record was the most powerful concert experience that I've ever been a part of," said Chaz Corzine, who managed Smith at the time. "Everybody knew we'd captured something really, really special."

They did indeed capture lightning in a bottle. Everyone there, from the artists to the fans, knew this was a history-making concert. Even Smith—the inspiration behind the concert—was stunned when it was all over.

"I remember going backstage and sitting down with everybody, and we all just started to cry," Smith said. "I was like, 'What just happened out there? What just happened out there?'"

But there was another shock yet to come.

Worship was released on one of the worst days in American history. It came out on September 11, 2001.

For such a time as this.

It was a smash.

Worship sold sixty thousand copies in the first week and even charted Top 20 on *Billboard*'s Album Charts. It eventually sold more than two million copies, was the best-selling CCM album of 2001, and is the second best-selling CCM album of all-time. *Worship* also received a 2002 Dove Award for Best Praise and Worship Album of the Year, and "Above All" won Inspirational Song of the Year.

It was the best-selling album of Smith's entire career and the easiest to make. But it was more than just an album; it was perhaps a brief glimpse of what heaven might be like.

"There was something about that record . . . 9/11," Smith said. "I think it was a go-to for people."

People were buying *Worship* by the case and sharing it with all of their friends. Was it a sign of the times? Smith certainly thought so.

"There's a real hunger for God in people's lives, particularly in the younger generation," Smith said. "There's this resurgence of something happening to people, and that's why praise and worship music is so popular."

WORSHIP, MICHAEL W. SMITH (2001, REUNION RECORDS) RELEASED ON SEPTEMBER 11, 2001. IT IS THE SECOND BEST-SELLING ALBUM IN CCM HISTORY.

It was more than popular; it was the catalyst for the worship music explosion in the decade that followed.

A flood of praise albums hit the market. The same month *Worship* dropped, the English band Delirious? released *Deeper: The D:finite Worship Experience. In the Company of Angels: A Call to Worship* by Caedmon's Call also appeared on shelves next to these two releases.

The genre never really died. Integrity Music released a whole slew of worship albums, including the Hosana! Music series in the early 1980s. They later morphed into Integrity Publishers and Integrity Media in the early 2000s.

While worship music was the newest and latest thing, it also had ties that hearkened to the Jesus Movement on Southern California beaches.

IT WAS THE CATALYST FOR THE WORSHIP MUSIC EXPLOSION IN THE DECADE THAT FOLLOWED.

JOEL HOUSTON, FOUNDING MEMBER OF HILLSONG UNITED, STARTED AS AN EAGER TEENAGER ON HILLSONG CHURCH'S YOUTH WORSHIP TEAM IN SYDNEY, AUSTRALIA. HE WAS DEEPLY INSPIRED BY SONGS FROM PASSIONATE BANDS LIKE DELIRIOUS?. HILLSONG RELEASED ITS FIRST YOUTH ALBUM IN 2005.

TODAY, HILLSONG UNITED IS A ROTATING GROUP OF MUSICIANS AND WORSHIP LEADERS WHO TOUR THE WORLD LEADING STADIUMS OF PEOPLE IN WORSHIP.

It was something K-LOVE CEO Bill Reeves instantly recognized.

"You look back at artists like Larry Norman, Sweet Comfort Band, and the REZ band, and I think you'll find elements of praise music, even during the Jesus Movement," Reeves said.

He wasn't the only one to pick up on the similarities.

"It's interesting that you'll find the first wave of Christian music was called Jesus Music," said Greg Laurie. "That says a lot right there. It was Jesus Music, and it was a Jesus Movement. Then it became Contemporary Christian music, and there wasn't a lot said about Jesus. But what I really love about worship music is that it's going back to Jesus."

In a way, it was back to its roots where performance was about passion rather than professionalism. Back to the days when the artists weren't worried about chart performance, distribution, or marketing. Worship and praise artists were more concerned about putting on a great service than dressing a showcase window.

"These songs were making their way into churches, and it was this real, beautiful grassroots thing," said Chris Tomlin, who became the breakout star of the genre. "No publishers, no labels and all of these other things. Just these churches passing their songs around."

While all this seemed very down to earth and a return to basics, it was characterized by the rise of stadium-sized events replete with lasers, light banks, smoke, and major engagement with the audience.

Louie Giglio—pastor of Atlanta's Passion City Church, where Chris Tomlin and Matt Redman started out—said, "These big stadium events started happening, and all of a sudden there was something new in the air."

The music didn't stay at home. It migrated around the world to places like England and Australia, where Delirious? and Hillsong became household names. Hillsong's lead singer, Joel Houston, thought that every church played music and wrote their own songs.

"The songs are now the church and have taken off around the world," Houston said. "There was no grand plan there. There were also rumors of our songs being played from our church and being played around the world."

THE MUSIC DIDN'T STAY AT HOME. IT MIGRATED AROUND THE WORLD.

The influence was stronger than anyone suspected, even to people like Giglio who, in his own way, was a pioneer of this new movement.

"We had heard about Hillsong because 'Shout to the Lord' had become the biggest song in the church," Giglio said. "Then all of a sudden we started realizing there was something percolating in England . . . this Delirious? band had been on the scene doing something that no one has ever done before. They're creating a band sound."

Worship bands had created new rock concerts but with a lot more audience participation and without weed or whiskey. And they were just as loud and energetic as a Who or Led Zeppelin show.

"The sound of the people singing over the top of us was deafening," Houston said. "I remember stepping back from the microphone and watching these people sing these songs, like so loud that I didn't have to sing."

He didn't need to.

Hearts were hungry, and people were desperate. They were tired of the status quo and wanted a fresh encounter with God. Worship and praise music was the new gateway.

Leading the charge was Grammy and Dove Award-winning artist Chris Tomlin, an unassuming singer-songwriter and worship leader from Grand Saline, Texas. So unassuming, in fact, he didn't see himself leading anything.

"I think that's where the worship music, the explosion of it in the early days, [wasn't] driven by a personality but because they were connecting to

God," Tomlin said. "They didn't wonder who wrote these songs; it wasn't about that. The early days were so special in that way."

Michael W. Smith created an experience in the early 2000s with his worship records. Then Chris Tomlin took it to a whole new level and perfected it. *TIME* magazine agreed with Tomlin that it was about the songs and not the singer.

"People sing his songs a lot, often repeatedly. Specifically, they sing them in church," noted *TIME* reporter Belinda Luscombe in a 2006 piece. "According to Christian Copyright Licensing International (CCLI), an organization that licenses music to churches, Tomlin, 34, is the most often sung contemporary artist in U.S. congregations every week. Since glee clubs have fallen out of popularity, that might make Tomlin the most often sung artist anywhere."

That would be more than the Beatles, Elton John, or any other superstars of music.

Tomlin had laid a foundation. Chris Tomlin songs were much bigger than Chris Tomlin. A whole new generation of artists took that experience to places no one thought possible. Artists like Hillsong, Bethel, Casting Crowns, Kari Jobe, Phil Wickham, Jesus Culture, Third Day, and Elevation became the modern worship explosion.

Worship music was now a part of every Christian gathering from church services, concert halls, conferences, and crusades. People saw worship music as an opportunity to create a space to connect with the deepest of deeps within them. Modern worship singer Kari Jobe saw that firsthand.

"Music could shift a whole atmosphere and help people get on their face before God," said Jobe. "See, we're created for the eternal. We're created for the sacred."

It was like a tsunami. Worship and praise albums became best sellers. Worship acts were almost as big as Amy Grant and Stryper in their heydays. Concerts were mostly sell-out affairs. Everyone felt the value of worship. Something there resonated within their spirits more than anything else did.

"I think it was just one of those moments where the spirit of God globally was answering the prayers of people," Giglio said.

"MUSIC COULD SHIFT A WHOLE ATMOSPHERE AND HELP PEOPLE GET ON THEIR FACE BEFORE GOD."

KING OF FOOLS, DELIRIOUS? (1997, FURIOUS RECORDS) INCLUDES THEIR BEST KNOWN SONG, "HISTORY MAKER."

Formerly of Passion City Church, Matt Redman, one of the most successful worship songwriters of the era, felt that when God moves, it's accompanied by a soundtrack.

"And so often it's not the soundtrack that releases the thing, it's just that God's moving, and there's this musical outburst because of what God's doing," Redman said.

Tomlin said no one should get the credit for this explosion. It belonged to someone else.

"Music is God's idea," Tomlin said. "Let's not forget where all of this came from."

Smith attributed the origin of that power to divine mystery.

"Music is the most powerful universal language in the world, like how a three-and-a-half-minute song can change somebody's life," Smith said. "It's just extraordinary to me. Or how you can play an instrumental, play a melody, and start crying. I mean, there's no words. It's a mystery."

A genre had been born, grown up, evolved, changed, collapsed in upon itself, and had grown again. It was about to achieve a sort of equilibrium.

A NEW ERA OF WORSHIP LEADERS AND ARTISTS RISES UP. FROM LEFT TO RIGHT: JENN JOHNSON, TAUREN WELLS, JEKALYN CARR, CHRISTINE D'CLARIO, TOGETHER AT THE 2020 DOVE AWARDS.

CHAPTER 13

KEEPING THE FIRE

On the rolling, wooded hills outside Nashville, Tennessee, there's a farm nestled in the woods. Three cabins from the 1800s, a barn, and an outhouse sit at the top of a grassy slope. The farm has electricity, but no running water. Usually, it's pretty quiet. The only sounds are blue jays, Carolina chickadees, wood thrushes, Eastern meadowlarks, and the breeze whispering in the trees.

"Yeah, a farmer that does a little music on the side," she replied with a mischievous smile.

It's a special place to Grant, who visits when she needs a break to recharge her creative batteries. Things are slow here, and one of the first things she does is slip on her snake boots and walk the grounds. She and Vince Gill got married at the locale in 2000. Her mother's ashes are buried there. A few years ago, her sister Cathy started keeping

KEEPING THE FIRE

It's not very different from the rural South before the Civil War. But today this spot is a haven for musicians and artists to write, relax, contemplate, heal, and step back from their relentless obligations.

"It's beautiful to have a place, but it's even more beautiful if you share it," says the farmer.

The farmer's name is Amy Grant. She hosts day camps during the summers. One year she held music lessons, and a little boy came up to her and said, "I thought you were the farmer."

bees at the site. It's also a place where Grant started a special tradition.

Every January 1 since 2017, logs are kindled in the firepit. The flames burn until the spring, sometimes roaring with fresh fuel, sometimes barely glowing in the early morning chill, but alive enough to jump back with a bit of tending.

"What if everybody needs a fire?" Grant said. "What if everybody needs something as simple as a flame to hold them in place so they can process their life?"

Grant absently stared into the flames and said the first thing that popped into her head.

"Things become beautiful because you nurture them," she said.

Contemporary Christian music has been nurtured and tended to for more than a half-century. All types of artists have "walked up to the fire and added some fuel," after Larry Norman struck the first match. Some stoked it into a Viking funeral

actually dealing with. You don't have to be Christian to relate to them."

Fittingly, reincarnation has become a story in the past decade. With their dynamic style, Victorian military coats, and backdrops of crashing waves and burning ships, for KING & COUNTRY is in some ways an homage to the theatrical acts of the eighties like Stryper. Amy Grant has passed her mantle on to Lauren Daigle, with her fresh-faced

pyre, and some have slipped in enough sticks for a small, primitive cooking fire. Rock, pop, rap, metal, gospel, country, alternative, praise and worship—they've all had their time in the limelight over the past five decades.

Some artists have bridged the secular and the sacred worlds with their music. NF is labeled as a Christian rapper, but he doesn't see himself that way.

"I'm a Christian, but I don't make Christian music," he said. "You're not going to reach everyone with just one point of view. I write about things I'm

star power.

Michael W. Smith holds up an album of Lauren Daigle and makes the same comparison.

"So Amy back in the day was the new kid on the block and just exploded," Smith said. "Here's Lauren Daigle, and she's the new kid on the block."

Grant agrees and sees so much of Daigle in her.

"I really like Lauren," she said. "Right as her rocket ship was ignited, I was like, 'Do you wanna go walk and sit in the woods?'"

AMY GRANT'S FARM OUTSIDE NASHVILLE
SERVES AS A GETAWAY FOR MUSICIANS WHO
NEED PEACE AND A PLACE FOR REFLECTION.

That talk wasn't a polite, getting-to-know-you chitchat. It was about how to handle stardom and stay grounded.

"She [Grant] told me, 'The first purchase you need to make is a piece of property because you need the place for solace,'" Daigle said. "And I think she recognized that she and I are wired so similarly. I've been to that cabin [Grant's], and it is so perfectly simple. There's not much to it. You play games, and you write a note. And you light a fire."

The torch has been passed and will continue to be passed.

Many of the folks from the Jesus Music and early CCM eras have gone on to glory to join the eternal choir, worshipping God. Larry Norman. Andraé Crouch. Keith Green. Rich Mullins. Carman Licciardello. Dana Key. Jonathan Pierce. And most recently, B.J. Thomas.

Some remain to tell the story; fewer still are involved in the industry. When they look back, they talk about making music because they didn't know at the time that they were making history.

"People would say, 'You're a pioneer,'" said Matthew Ward of 2nd Chapter of Acts. "Well, you don't know you're a pioneer when you're doing it."

That was a bonus.

These dreamers, entrepreneurs, and pioneers didn't know they were helping to create an entire industry. In fact, very few recognize the enormity of the price paid by the early Christian artists and how they shaped a movement from dust. The best

they had were record label support and limited radio. They didn't have today's technological tools or social media to boost their artistry, profile, or music. Back in the not-so-distant past, streaming services like Spotify, Apple Music, or Pandora did not exist. Neither did YouTube, which has minted more than a few CCM stars since its 2005 debut. And the only church that self-published its own albums was Maranatha! Music. Today, to self-publish is commonplace, and the production values and money spent on these ventures can rival the differences between a NASA mission and a model plane.

These pioneers are truly the unsung heroes of the Christian music past. In fact, if you look closely at the survivors, you can still see a quiet flame in their eyes—a flame that at the time before recognition, rewards, money, and acceptance were

SOME REMAIN TO TELL THE STORY; FEWER STILL ARE INVOLVED IN THE INDUSTRY.

byproducts of their creativity, burned so intensely that they were greatly responsible for the powerful "fire in the belly" of those great artists who followed and built upon that foundation.

These old-timers were the ones who slept five people in a van, slated two people to a gyro sandwich, and in return for their lyrical ministry, received a paltry few dollars from a lonely collection plate as an honorarium for their dedication and sacrifice. There were no tour buses, trophies, nice hotels, or accolades from sold-out crowds. There were, though, spouses who worked to pay the rent, as well as kids at home who saw tired mommies and daddies resting up from the rugged road just so they could go back to singing about the "Old Rugged Cross" to hurting souls. These people responded like modern-day Jeremiahs to God's calling, dedicating their very being to his purpose. They had no idea about the groundwork they were laying and what it would mean to millions one day, though they would have done it anyway! When Jesus tugged on their arms and said, "Let's go," he also hugged their hearts, and that's all they needed to know. Serving God's purpose in return for his gracious gift of talent was what it was all about then. In its own way, that purpose is what it's still all about today.

Sixstepsrecords label owner Louie Giglio is heartened by the new wave of CCM artists, saying, "We're now in a transition zone of wanting to pass on the baton to a new generation, to say, 'Okay, now you run. And you go and watch what God can do.'"

The beauty of today's CCM world is that new artists continue to embrace it, TobyMac said. "The

Lecraes and Lauren Daigles of the world . . . these people are just out there," he said. "They're not put under the category of Christian music."

Secular artists are starting to feel the same way. When Joel and Luke Smallbone of for KING & COUNTRY remixed their song "God Only Knows" to include country legend Dolly Parton, she leapt at the chance to dip her toe in the CCM pool. She was looking for more faith-based material to record. The song and video hit like a tidal wave. It sailed to No. 2 on the Billboard Hot Christian songs charts and rested there for an astounding nineteen weeks. It also landed on the Billboard Hot 100 chart, making

"WE'RE NOW IN A TRANSITION ZONE OF WANTING TO PASS ON THE BATON TO A NEW GENERATION."

it for KING & COUNTRY's first such crossover hit. A 2020 Grammy nomination for Best Contemporary Christian Music Performance/Song was the cherry on top for this inspired collaboration.

Kanye West's recent and not-so-quiet conversion resulted in his "Sunday Services," which looked like pop-up worship events throughout the country. These impromptu but highly stylized concerts tapped into a spiritual vein that showed today's youth are not totally done with Christianity. *Jesus Is King* debuted at No. 1 on *Billboard*'s Top 200 album chart in October 2019. Listeners were surprised, and this resulted in an even bigger surprise when it garnered the Best Contemporary Christian Music Album award at the 2021 Grammys. West called it "an expression of the gospel," and this album signaled a significant change in the artist's life.

Like West, artist Justin Bieber also underwent a spiritual metamorphosis, which impacted his life and music. His Easter surprise EP *Freedom* was released in April 2021 and also raced to the top of the charts. The EP, which included a "3:16" timestamp on the cover, "is the first instance of the artist situating an entire project in an unapologetically Christian framework," according to the Religion News Service.

Not to be outdone, country artist Carrie Underwood also recorded her first album of gospel hymns in 2021. *My Savior* consisted of traditional gospel hymns Underwood grew up

"MUSIC DOES CARRY THE HOPE OF THE GOSPEL."

singing ("Jesus Loves Me," "Just As I Am," "How Great Thou Art," etc.) and features a duet ("Great Is Thy Faithfulness") with CCM star CeCe Winans. Her label, Capitol Records Nashville, went big and gave *My Savior* a digital, compact disc, and vinyl release and also offered it as a limited-edition box set.

Regardless of where these mainstream and top-selling artist are in their faith, their choices and their successes demonstrate how God is continuing to move through people in different ways, essentially using these crooked sticks to draw straight lines and push CCM into new territory.

There's a passage in the Book of Isaiah: "And from them I will send survivors" (66:19 ESV). That's the legacy of Jesus Music—that it has changed, survived, and thrived.

"Every setback, there will be a glimmer of hope," Lecrae said. "Every time the walls just keep coming up, a brick would fall."

In the end, we are left with the question of why.

Greg Laurie said it's because Christian music lifts you up. "I think people desperately need hope right now because we're living in what can appear like hopeless times," he said.

Hillsong musician Joel Houston agreed.

"Music can sustain us in the toughest of times," he said. "That's a gift from God."

Lauren Daigle uses her music to worship God. She feels her connection with him through that. "When I think about the Christian music space, I think it's beautiful, and I think it has a purpose," she said. "Music does carry the hope of the gospel."

That is why CCM continues to thrive.

"My profound hope is that this music continues to reach out around the world more than ever in history and offers people a sense of hope and a sense of togetherness and a sense of joy maybe that they have not experienced," said Joel Smallbone of for KING & COUNTRY.

Don't forget: It's rock, which means there's some amount of orneriness and rebellion in there. Michael Sweet captured that when he said, "Stryper's still going and going, and we're going to keep going until we're not here any longer. That might frustrate some people because some may wish we were."

Without doubt, CCM has had its setbacks, but it continues to push forward. Crossover star CeCe Winans said she's honored to be a part of it and doesn't take that honor lightly.

"I think we've come a long way, and I still think we have a ways to go in really becoming family," Winans said. "We're stronger together. We're a force to be reckoned with. I think we're going to make a stronger impact on a world that desperately needs us."

Over a half-century later, legendary guitarist, multiple Dove Award recipient, and Gospel Music Hall of Fame inductee Phil Keaggy is still traveling those same back roads and crowded highways, performing at everything from church picnics to Carnegie Hall. Like Amy Grant, he has that all-consuming fire that keeps burning and warming souls, young and old.

The fire is still being kept. Down the road, many more will surely throw logs on it, keeping the flame strong. Hope continues to be stoked. So it will be for the next fifty years. Or more.

Why? Because the inspiration for this music will not change. The reason for these music makers and lyricists to do what they do isn't going anywhere. He is the same . . . yesterday, today, forever (Hebrews 13:8).

Jesus rocks.

Can he get an amen?

THE 2019 K-LOVE FAN AWARDS. FROM LEFT TO RIGHT: MANDISA, LAUREN DAIGLE, MATTHEW WEST.

MICHAEL W. SMITH AT THE 20TH ANNIVERSARY RE-RECORDING OF THE *WORSHIP* ALBUM. *WORSHIP FOREVER*, A RE-IMAGINING OF THE 2001 ALBUM, WAS PERFORMED IN FRONT OF A LIVE AUDIENCE WITH A FULL SYMPHONY ORCHESTRA AT LIPSCOMB UNIVERSITY'S ALLEN ARENA ON JULY 12, 2021 IN NASHVILLE.

ACKNOWLEDGMENTS

This book came together at warp speed, and I was given a three-month deadline to finish the product you hold in your hands. A challenge indeed, but I've learned that challenges keep your blood circulating and you on your toes. This project, in many ways, has been one of the biggest thrill rides of my writing career.

Despite what you may think, writing is not a singular endeavor or isolated occupation—at least, not for me. I take a team approach when writing books. I surround myself with good people whom I trust to give input, guidance, contributions, and strong opinions. I didn't lack for any of those things when it came to assembling *The Jesus Music*.

First and foremost, I must thank the talented Erwin Brothers, who suggested me to adopt this companion book for their documentary, *The Jesus Music*. They made the writing of this book easy by making the subject matter compelling. Jon and Andy are not only impressive filmmakers, but these two people are good men and dedicated Christian

storytellers—in fact, they are the best in the business.

Thanks also goes to Scott Seckel, my developmental editor, who spent many weekends with me helping to shape this manuscript and doing "Western Union-style" writing in order to meet the deadline. Joshua Walsh of Kingdom Story Company, who produced *The Jesus Music*. and shaped the overall arc of what you see on the screen, spoon-fed me this story and answered all of my questions regarding all the players in the Contemporary Christian music pantheon. Greg Laurie, author, filmmaker, and senior pastor of Harvest Christian Fellowship, also chipped in as an editor/contributor, as did my literary agents, Erik and Robert Wolgemuth, and record executive, producer, friend, and eagle eye Ken Mansfield. I even enlisted my mom, Carolyn Terrill, who listened to Andraé Crouch, Evie Tornquist, and Bill Gaither and took me to Christian bookstores in my youth, giving me a baseline knowledge for this book. Giving the manuscript a final sheen was editor Cara Highsmith, who can be trusted to cross all the i's, dot all the t's, and get those pesky commas in the right place. She can also be counted on to tell me when I've crossed the line, which is often!

After the manuscript was delivered, a new team took over. In no particular order, that team included Brian Mitchell, David Schroeder, Matt West, Kathryn Notestine, Rachel Ryan, Jocelyn Bailey, Grace Carey-Hill, Brian Smith, and Sarah Siegand.

Special thanks to Will Turpin of Collective Soul, a longtime friend who helped me understand the rock side of the industry, while Petra's John Schlitt helped me understand the CCM side. Both were kind to offer their help.

And a special thanks must go to all the CCM artists and behind-the-scenes players who kept the fire going all these years.

Marshall Terrill
June 2021

NOTES

Chapter One

- "The experiment of drugs . . ." Tommy Coomes, personal interview, July 13, 2020.

- "My generation had seen . . ." Glenn Kaiser, personal interview, July 2, 2020.

- "My philosophy was that . . ." Chuck Girard, personal interview, July 13, 2020.

- "In the sixties, our heroes . . ." Greg Laurie, personal interview, September 4, 2020.

- "Larry Norman, who most . . ." John J. Thompson, personal interview, July 23, 2020.

- "Sloppy thinking, dishonest metaphors . . ." Harriet Veitch, "Rocker asked: why should the devil have all the good music?" *Sydney Morning Herald*, April 22, 2008.

- "The early stuff he put out . . ." John Styll, personal interview, July 24, 2020.

- "Only a Christian on the stage . . ." David Di Sabatino, *Fallen Angel: The Outlaw Larry Norman*, Jester Media, 2009.

- "Was he a complicated . . ." John J. Thompson, personal interview, July 23, 2020.

- "Some people felt he . . ." John Styll, personal interview, July 24, 2020.

- "Larry was a photographer . . ." John Styll, personal interview, July 24, 2020.

- "I'd known Larry better . . ." Glenn Kaiser, personal interview, June 2, 2020.

- "You could be famous . . ." Terry Mattingly, "Larry Norman and the wars over 'Christian' music and art," *Knoxville News Sentinel*, April 21, 2018.

- "My dad has always . . ." Mike Norman, personal interview, October 2, 2020.

- "It wasn't really a . . ." Greg Laurie, personal interview, September 4, 2020.

- "Larry is the single . . ." Chuck Girard, personal interview, July 13, 2020.

- "I find it hard to admit . . ." Ken Mansfield, personal interview, May 1, 2021.

Chapter Two

- "Sincere love for strangers . . ." *Chuck Smith Jr., A Memoir of Grace* (Costa Mesa, California: The Word For Today, 2009), 17.

- "We had paid a price . . ." *Chuck Smith Jr., A Memoir of Grace*, 151.

- "You know, they are desperately . . ." Jim Daly, "Remembering Pastor Chuck Smith," *Daly Focus*, October 4, 2013.

- "I went through Haight-Ashbury . . ." Chuck Girard, personal interview, July 13, 2020.

- "We have to meet . . ." *Chuck Smith Jr., A Memoir of Grace,* 157.
- "He would put us down . . ." *Lonnie Frisbee and Roger Sachs, Not by Might, Nor by Power: The Jesus Revolution Part One* (Santa Maria, California: Freedom Publications, 2017), 49.
- "It was like when John Lennon . . ." *Greg Laurie and Ellen Vaughn, Jesus Revolution: How God Transformed an Unlikely Generation and How He Can Do It Again Today* (Ada, Michigan: Baker Books, 2018), 76.
- "Their hearts were so filled," Dan Wooding, "Jesus Has Never Stopped Moving!!!" *Assist News Service,* https://calvary-sanclemente.org/home-2/jesus-revolution/.
- "I walked inside . . ." *Chuck Girard, Rock & Roll Preacher* (Houston, Texas: World Wide Publishing Group, 2021), 133.
- "Within a few weeks . . ." Tommy Coomes, personal interview, July 13, 2020.
- "We have our guitars . . ." Ken Mansfield and Marshall Terrill, *Rock and a Heart Place: A Rock 'n' Roller-coaster Ride from Rebellion to Sweet Salvation* (Nashville, Tennessee: BroadStreet Publishers, 2015).
- "I was fearful . . ." Erika I. Ritchie, "Chuck Smith, Calvary Chapel founder, dies after cancer battle," *Orange County Register,* October 4, 2013.

Chapter Three

- "It is a startling development . . ." "The Alternative Jesus: Psychedelic Christ," *TIME,* June 21, 1971.
- "When I first attended . . ." Greg Laurie, personal interview, September 4, 2020.
- "How were we going . . ." Tommy Coomes, personal interview, July 13, 2020.
- "Andraé was probably one . . ." Bill Gaither, personal interview, June 26, 2020.
- "The very first concert . . ." Steven Curtis Chapman, personal interview, June 2, 2020.
- "I think that when we . . ." Christopher Dean Hopkins, "Andraé Crouch, 'Father of Modern Gospel,' Dies," *NPR,* January 8, 2015.
- "I remember I walked . . ." Michael W. Smith, personal interview, April 27, 2020.
- "The stuff, honestly, wasn't . . ." John Styll, personal interview, July 24, 2020.
- "We literally put those . . ." Tommy Coomes, personal interview, July 13, 2020.
- "For me, the key thing . . ." Chuck Girard, personal interview, July 13, 2020.

Chapter Four

- "Pat Boone took a tremendous . . ." Chris Christian, personal interview, May 5, 2021.
- "I just happened to be . . ." Chris Christian, personal interview, May 5, 2021.
- "He implemented a . . ." Jesse Carey, "11 Keith Green Songs That Changed Worship Music," *Relevant,* July 28, 2015.
- "He [Lennon] was watching . . ." Bob Rosen, personal interview, April 15, 2021.
- "A knee-buckling experience . . ." Andrew McCarron, "The year Bob Dylan was born again: a timeline," *Oxford*

University Press Blog, January 21, 2017.

- "Jesus put his hand on me . . ." Andrew McCarron.

- "'Gotta Serve Somebody' . . ." Jaan Uhelszki, "Taped 'Diary' of John Lennon Unearthed," *Rolling Stone*, April 1, 1999.

Chapter Five

- "When I realized . . ." Amy Grant, personal interview, May 14, 2020.

- "I thought, Man . . ." Amy Grant, personal interview, May 14, 2020.

- "Look, Amy, I have . . ." Brown Bannister, personal interview, September 9, 2020.

- "She's not that great . . ." *Amy Grant, Mosaic: Pieces of My Life So Far* (New York, New York: Crown, 2008), 45.

- "It was a different time . . ." Dan Armonaitis, "Amy Grant, Steven Curtis Chapman end tour in Greenville," *Spartanburg Herald-Journal*, February 25, 2016.

- "It [Amy Grant] had kind of . . ." John Styll, personal interview, July 24, 2020.

- "It was both a vanguard . . ." John Styll, personal interview, July 24, 2020.

- "Man's physical and spiritual . . ." Jane Menninga, "New FM Station," *Lincoln-Journal Star*, March 16, 1975.

- "It was almost a . . ." *Paul Baker, Contemporary Christian Music: Where It Came from, What It Is, and Where It's Going.* (Westchester, Illinois: Crossway Books, 1985), 94.

- "The FCCM was born . . ." Paul Baker, 94.

Chapter Six

- "A lot of my concerts . . ." B.J. Thomas, qtd. in Steve Morse, "Jesus Rock explodes: new medium, old message," *The Boston Globe*, July 10, 1982.

- "The problem I have . . ." Kerry Livgren, qtd. in "Jesus Rock explodes."

- "Some Christian acts do . . ." Dan Russell, qtd. in "Jesus Rock explodes."

- "I think the reason why . . ." John J. Thompson, personal interview, July 23, 2020.

- "He'd have an idea . . ." Amy Grant, personal interview, May 14, 2020.

- "I wouldn't be sitting . . ." Michael W. Smith, personal interview, April 27, 2020.

- "If it wasn't for them . . ." John J. Thompson, personal interview, July 23, 2020.

Chapter Seven

- "You have your pop . . ." Greg Laurie, personal interview, September 4, 2020.

- "Anytime your face . . ." John Styll, personal interview, July 24, 2020.

- "Home and hearth become . . ." *Ken Mansfield and Marshall Terrill, Rock and a Heart Place: A Rock 'n' Roller-coaster*

Ride from Rebellion to Sweet Salvation (Nashville, Tennessee: BroadStreet Publishers, 2015, pg. 255.

- "Satan is so good . . ." John Schlitt, personal interview, April 14, 2021.

- "Back in the 1980s . . ." John J. Thompson, personal interview, July 23, 2020.

- "We don't talk about . . ." Andraé Crouch, qtd. in Lee Hildebrand, "A Religious Rocker Ticks Off the Christians," *San Francisco Examiner*, August 10, 1986.

- "I got my humor . . ." Russ Taff, personal interview, June 25, 2020.

- "You're not worth . . ." Russ Taff, personal interview, June 25, 2020.

- "My body demanded that . . ." Russ Taff, personal interview, June 25, 2020.

- "If we were to take . . ." John Styll, personal interview, July 24, 2020.

- "We got along like . . ." Amy Grant, qtd. in Jay Orr, "Amy Grant prepares for new tour – and new life," *Tennessean*, October 25, 1999.

- "A lot of disparaging . . ." Amy Grant, qtd. in Jay Orr, "Amy Grant prepares."

- "The Christian community . . ." John Styll, personal interview, July 24, 2020.

- "I never thought I . . ." Amy Grant, qtd. in Jay Orr, "Amy Grant prepares."

- "If there's anything dark . . ." Michael W. Smith, personal interview, April 27, 2020.

- "I couldn't even find . . ." Amy Grant, personal interview, May 14, 2020.

- "I had an affair . . ." Sandi Patty, qtd. in Paul Reinhard, "Christian singer who rose, fell quickly is rising again," *The Morning Call*, November 5, 1998.

- "I had exhausted every avenue . . ." Michael English, qtd. in Deborah Evans Price, "Q&A – After bottoming out, Michael English 'Comes Home,'" *Reuters*, March 15, 2008.

- "I think Christian artists . . ." Al Andrews, personal interview, July 16, 2020.

- "People are not looking . . ." Greg Laurie, personal interview, September 4, 2020.

Chapter Eight

- "The metal scene in . . ." John J. Thompson, personal interview, July 23, 2020.

- "I said, 'Probably are . . ." Bill Gaither, personal interview, June 26, 2020.

- "Christian metal wasn't part . . ." John J. Thompson, personal interview, July 23, 2020.

- "The established church wanted . . ." John Styll, personal interview, July 24, 2020.

- "It was brand-new . . ." Steve Taylor, personal interview, June 15, 2020.

- "If you've ever heard . . ." John Cooper, personal interview, July 1, 2020.

- "The church didn't really . . ." Eddie DeGarmo, personal interview, June 15, 2020.

- "Petra was the first . . ." Chris Tomlin, personal interview, September 8, 2020.

- "My mom gave me . . ." John Cooper, personal interview, July 1, 2020.

- "I thought that the . . ." John Schlitt, personal interview, April 14, 2021.

- "They didn't help one . . ." John Schlitt, personal interview, April 14, 2021.

- "I ignore them because . . ." John Schlitt, personal interview, April 14, 2021.

- "I remember standing . . ." John Schlitt, personal interview, April 14, 2021.

- "Stryper had such a . . ." Joel Smallbone, personal interview, June 22, 2020.

- "Stryper comes on . . ." John Cooper, personal interview, July 1, 2020.

- "They had a big part . . ." Ken Mansfield interview, May 1, 2021.

- "Demons, worshippers, covens . . ." Michael Guido, personal interview, June 18, 2020.

- "I see them at a . . ." John J. Thompson, personal interview, July 23, 2020.

- "The thing about them . . ." John Styll, personal interview, July 24, 2020.

- "Literally, Jimmy pretty much . . ." Michael Sweet, personal interview, June 29, 2020.

- "Things were happening . . ." Michael Sweet, personal interview, June 29, 2020.

- "Once the band made . . ." Michael Sweet, personal interview, June 29, 2020.

- "Jimmy was holding up . . ." Mylon LeFevre, personal interview, October 15, 2020.

- "Rejection from the world . . ." Mylon LeFevre, personal interview, October 15, 2020.

- "People were quitting the . . ." Mylon LeFevre, personal interview, October 15, 2020.

- "In my view, music . . ." Stan Moser, *We Will Stand: The Real Story Behind the Songs, Artists & Executives that Built the Contemporary Christian Music Industry* (Brentwood, Tennessee: CCM United, 2015), 149.

Chapter Nine

- "Old dividing walls between . . ." Amy Grant, personal interview, May 14, 2020.

- "I remember there being . . ." John J. Thompson, personal interview, July 23, 2020.

- "I said, 'You know . . ." Eddie DeGarmo, personal interview, June 15, 2020.

- "God forbid they have . . ." Natalie Grant, personal interview, July 28, 2020.

- "I could tell that . . ." Michael W. Smith, personal interview, April 27, 2020.

- "Today it's a different . . ." Michael W. Smith, personal interview, April 27, 2020.

- "I don't remember who . . ." Michael W. Smith, personal interview, April 27, 2020.

- "Working in Smith's favor . . ." Steve Hochman, "Smith brings vitality to his Gospel Pitch," *Los Angeles Times*, March 29, 1993.

- "'Flood' was crazy . . ." Dan Haseltine, personal interview, July 16, 2020.

- "The whole experience was . . ." Leigh Nash, personal interview, September 9, 2020.

- "You could maybe make . . ." Steve Taylor, personal interview, June 15, 2020.

- "Everything just got bigger . . ." John Styll, personal interview, July 24, 2020.

- "What happened in the . . ." John J. Thompson, personal interview, July 23, 2020.

- "There was a huge changing . . ." Eddie DeGarmo, personal interview, June 15, 2020.

- "It was such an exciting . . ." Steven Curtis Chapman, personal interview, June 2, 2020.

- "Our goal was not . . ." Dan Haseltine, personal interview, July 16, 2020.

- "You see a pretty rapid . . ." John J. Thompson, personal interview, July 23, 2020.

- "When Christian music first . . ." Steve Taylor, personal interview, June 15, 2020.

- "So now the industry . . ." John J. Thompson, personal interview, July 23, 2020.

Chapter Ten

- "I sang in chapel . . ." Michael Tait, personal interview, June 1, 2020.

- "We had this little . . ." TobyMac, personal interview, May 27, 2020.

- "We'd get up and . . ." Michael Tait, personal interview, June 1, 2020.

- "We went to see . . ." TobyMac, personal interview, May 27, 2020.

- "I remember them . . ." Kevin Max, personal interview, July 7, 2020.

- "Here's the deal . . ." Michael Tait, personal interview, June 1, 2020.

- "I didn't know . . ." TobyMac, personal interview, May 27, 2020.

- "We were just doing . . ." TobyMac, personal interview, May 27, 2020.

- "When we started . . ." Kevin Max, personal interview, July 7, 2020.

- "They were our roadies . . ." Eddie DeGarmo, personal interview, June 15, 2020.

- "I'd like for you . . ." TobyMac, personal interview, May 27, 2020.

- "I went to Billy . . ." Rick Marshall, qtd. in Harrison Metzger, "Graham Crusade events attract young people," *Blue Ridge Times-News*, July 24, 2001.

- "Music is the popular . . ." Rick Marshall, qtd. in Harrison Metzger, "Graham Crusade events attract young people."

- "I told him the youth . . ." Rick Marshall, qtd. in Harrison Metzger, "Graham Crusade events attract young people."

- "Okay, they do know . . ." Michael Tait, personal interview, June 1, 2020.

- "Billy was always ahead . . ." Greg Laurie, personal interview, September 4, 2020.

- "We are so grateful . . ." TobyMac, personal interview, May 27, 2020.

- "Ruth Graham said . . ." TobyMac, personal interview, May 27, 2020.

- "I remember showing up . . ." Michael W. Smith, personal interview, April 27, 2020.

- "Man, every memory . . ." Michael Tait, personal interview, June 1, 2020.

- "Billy received a resounding . . ." Greg Laurie, personal interview, September 4, 2020.

- "We ran out of . . ." Rick Marshall, qtd. in Harrison Metzger, "Graham Crusade events attract young people."
- "Outside of this . . ." TobyMac, personal interview, May 27, 2020.
- "Nobody was doing . . ." Michael W. Smith, personal interview, April 27, 2020.
- "Frankly, I'm surprised . . ." John Styll, personal interview, July 24, 2020.
- "I said, 'Kevin . . ." Michael Tait, personal interview, June 1, 2020.
- "DC Talk takes the . . ." Richard Harrington, "Rolling On: The Word from DC Talk," *Washington Post*, April 13, 1994.
- "One time, Mike and . . ." Kevin Max, personal interview, July 7, 2020.
- "Fame simply boils down . . ." Will Turpin, personal interview, May 7, 2021.
- "You're stuck with . . ." Will Turpin, personal interview, May 7, 2021.
- "Yeah, there was tension . . ." Mark Stuart, personal interview, June 4, 2020.
- "I remember we were . . ." TobyMac, personal interview, May 27, 2020.
- "I don't look at . . ." Kevin Max, personal interview, July 7, 2020.
- "There's no question . . ." Bill Reeves, personal interview, April 16, 2020.
- "I remember the hole . . ." Kirk Franklin, personal interview, June 23, 2020.
- "I was a couple of . . ." Kirk Franklin, personal interview, June 23, 2020.
- "They played 'Stomp' . . ." Bone Hampton, personal interview, July 10, 2020.
- "Some people think . . ." John J. Thompson, personal interview, July 23, 2020.
- "It was a problem . . ." Kirk Franklin, personal interview, June 23, 2020.
- "'God, man . . . God . . ." Kirk Franklin, personal interview, June 23, 2020.
- "When it comes to . . ." Kirk Franklin, personal interview, June 23, 2020.
- "Kirk has been an . . ." John J. Thompson, personal interview, July 23, 2020.

Chapter Eleven

- "It was something that . . ." Shawn Fanning, qtd. in Stephen Dowling. "Napster turns 20: How it changed the music industry," *BBC*, May 31, 2019.
- "All the way back . . ." John J. Thompson, personal interview, July 23, 2020.
- "In the late '90s . . ." Hilary Rosen, qtd. in Ernesto Van der Sar. "How the MP3, Pirates and Apple Changed the Music Industry," *TorrentFreak*, January 17, 2021.
- "You know about . . ." Hilary Rosen, qtd. in "Business Wars: Napster vs. the Record Labels," *Wondery*, February 22, 2021.
- "Livin' La Vida Loca . . ." qtd. in "Business Wars."
- "'Bye Bye Bye' by NSYNC . . ." qtd. in "Business Wars."

- "Millions are listening . . ." Hilary Rosen, qtd. in "Business Wars."
- "I know it's illegal . . ." qtd. in Mike Drummond, "Evolving technology putting music lovers in ethical bind," *Charlotte Observer*, October 10, 2005.
- "There were lawsuits . . ." John Styll, personal interview, July 24, 2020.
- "We can sell more . . ." Ed Roland, qtd. in Dan Aquilante, "The Soul Survivors – Georgia Rockers Talk about Death, Divorce and Ditching their Record Label," *New York Post*, November 14, 2004.
- "We're having to hustle . . ." Ed Roland, qtd. in Seamus Gallivan, "Tell Me," *The Buffalo News*, September 2, 2005.
- "It's as if someone . . ." John J. Thompson, personal interview, July 23, 2020.
- "Statistically, the sales . . ." John Styll, personal interview, July 24, 2020.
- "It was in the Cool . . ." John Elefante, personal interview, June 16, 2014.
- "The funny thing to me . . ." Randy Stonehill, qtd. in Dave Trout, "Interview with Randy Stonehill," *Under the Radar*, November 15, 2013.
- "Record companies are . . ." Randy Stonehill, qtd. in Dave Trout, "Interview with Randy Stonehill."

Chapter Twelve

- "I didn't want to . . ." Michael W. Smith, personal interview, April 27, 2020.
- "I'm not going to . . ." Michael W. Smith, personal interview, April 27, 2020.
- "I heard this audible . . ." Michael W. Smith, personal interview, April 27, 2020.
- "Okay, I'm gonna . . ." Michael W. Smith, personal interview, April 27, 2020.
- "I said, 'I want . . .'" Michael W. Smith, personal interview, April 27, 2020.
- "About halfway through . . ." Michael W. Smith, personal interview, April 27, 2020.
- "The recording of that . . ." Chaz Corzine, personal interview, April 29, 2020.
- "I remember going backstage . . ." Michael W. Smith, personal interview, April 27, 2020.
- "There was something about . . ." Michael W. Smith, personal interview, April 27, 2020.
- "There's a real hunger . . ." Michael W. Smith, personal interview, April 27, 2020.
- "You look back at . . ." Bill Reeves, personal interview, April 16, 2020.
- "It's interesting that you'll . . ." Greg Laurie, personal interview, September 4, 2020.
- "These songs were making . . ." Chris Tomlin, personal interview, September 8, 2020.
- "These big stadium events . . ." Louie Giglio, personal interview, September 23, 2020.
- "The songs are now . . ." Joel Houston, personal interview, September 3, 2020.
- "We had heard about . . ." Louie Giglio, personal interview, September 23, 2020.
- "The sound of the . . ." Joel Houston, personal interview, September 3, 2020.

- "I think that's where . . ." Chris Tomlin, personal interview, September 8, 2020.

- "People sing his songs . . ." Belinda Luscombe, "Hip Hymns Are Him," *TIME*, November 19, 2006.

- "Music could shift . . ." Kari Jobe, personal interview, September 28, 2020.

- "I think it was . . ." Louie Giglio, personal interview, September 23, 2020.

- "And so often it's . . ." Matt Redman, personal interview, September 3, 2020.

- "Music is God's idea . . ." Chris Tomlin, personal interview, September 8, 2020.

- "Music is the most . . ." Michael W. Smith, personal interview, April 27, 2020.

Chapter Thirteen

- "It's beautiful to have a place . . ." Amy Grant, personal interview, May 14, 2020.

- "Yeah, a farmer that does . . ." Amy Grant, qtd. in Kaylee Hammond, "A Late Summer Catch-Up with Amy Grant," *Southern Living*, April 2015.

- "What if everybody needs . . ." Amy Grant, personal interview, May 14, 2020.

- "Things become beautiful . . ." Amy Grant, personal interview, May 14, 2020.

- "I'm a Christian, but . . ." NF, qtd. in Jessica McKinney. "What You Need to Know About NF, the Artist Who Beat Out Chance the Rapper for a No. 1 Album," *Complex*, August 5, 2019.

- "So Amy back in . . ." Michael W. Smith, personal interview, April 27, 2020.

- "I really like Lauren . . ." Amy Grant, personal interview, May 14, 2020.

- "She [Grant] told me. . ." Lauren Daigle, personal interview, July 31, 2020.

- "People would say . . ." Matthew Ward, personal interview, July 27, 2020.

- "We're now in a transition . . ." Louie Giglio, personal interview, September 23, 2020.

- "The Lecraes and Lauren Daigles . . ." TobyMac, personal interview, May 27, 2020.

- "Is the first instance of the artist . . ." Kathryn Post, "Justin Bieber's Easter surprise EP, 'Freedom,' adds to his Jesus-filled chapter," *Religion News Service*, April 7, 2021, https://religionnews.com/2021/04/07/justin-biebers-easter-surprise-ep-freedom-adds-to-his-jesus-filled-chapter.

- "Every setback, there will . . ." Lecrae, personal interview, July 8, 2020.

- "I think you can sum . . ." Greg Laurie, personal interview, September 4, 2020.

- "Music can sustain us . . ." Joel Houston, personal interview, September 3, 2020.

- "When I think about . . ." Lauren Daigle, personal interview, July 31, 2020.

- "My profound hope is . . ." Joel Smallbone, personal interview, June 22, 2020.

- "Stryper's still going . . ." Michael Sweet, personal interview, June 29, 2020.

- "I think we've come . . ." CeCe Winans, personal interview, June 12, 2020.

BIBLIOGRAPHY

Baker, Paul. *Contemporary Christian Music: Where It Came from, What It Is, and Where It's Going*. Westchester: Crossway Books, 1985.

Christian, Chris. *A Grandmother's Prayer: Moments in a Music Life*. Dallas: True Potential Inc., 2019.

English, Michael. *The Prodigal Comes Home: My Story of Failure and God's Story of Redemption*. Nashville: Thomas Nelson, 2008.

Grant, Amy. *Mosaic: Pieces of My Life So Far*. New York City: Crown, 2008.

Knopper, Steve. *Appetite for Self-Destruction: The Spectacular Crash of the Record Industry in the Digital Age*. New York City: Free Press, 2017.

Laurie, Greg and Ellen Vaughn. *Jesus Revolution: How God Transformed an Unlikely Generation and How He Can Do It Again Today*. Grand Rapids: Baker Books, 2018.

Mansfield, Ken and Marshall Terrill. *Rock and a Heart Place: A Rock 'n' Roller-coaster Ride from Rebellion to Sweet Salvation*. Nashville: BroadStreet Publishing Group, 2015.

Moser, Stan. *We Will Stand: The Real Story Behind the Songs, Artists & Executives that Built the Contemporary Christian Music Industry*. Brentwood: CCM United, 2015.

Rosen, Robert. *Nowhere Man: The Final Days of John Lennon*. New York City: Soft Skull Press, 2000.

Swaggart, Jimmy and Robert Paul Lamb. *Religious Rock 'n' Roll: A Wolf in Sheep's Clothing*. Baton Rouge: Jimmy Swaggart Ministries, 1987.

Thompson, John J. *Raised by Wolves: The Story of Christian Rock & Roll*. Toronto: ECW Press, 2000.

Thornbury, Gregory Alan. *Why Should the Devil Have All the Good Music?: Larry Norman and the Perils of Christian Rock*. New York City: Convergent Books, 2018.

INDEX

PHOTO CREDITS

PHOTO CREDITS

FROM THE CREATORS OF *I CAN ONLY IMAGINE*

AMY GRANT   MICHAEL W. SMITH   DC TALK   LAUREN DAIGLE   LECRAE   FOR KING & COUNTRY   HILLSONG UNITED   KIRK FRANKLIN   TOBYMAC

CeCe WINANS   CHRIS TOMLIN   MERCYME   STEVEN CURTIS CHAPMAN   NEWSBOYS   JOHN COOPER   AND MORE

THE
JESUS MUSIC
THE SOUNDTRACK OF A MOVEMENT

LIONSGATE PRESENTS A KINGDOM STORY COMPANY PRODUCTION IN ASSOCIATION WITH K-LOVE FILMS AND SOUTHLAND STUDIOS AN ERWIN BROTHERS FILM
"THE JESUS MUSIC" MUSIC SUPERVISOR JESS CHAMBERS EDITOR JOHN PUCKETT PARKER ADAMS DIRECTOR OF PHOTOGRAPHY KRISTOPHER S. KIMLIN PRODUCERS MICHAEL W. SMITH AMY GRANT
EXECUTIVE PRODUCERS ANDREW ERWIN JON ERWIN GREG HAM BILL REEVES JEFF VERDOORN TONY YOUNG KEVIN DOWNES PRODUCED BY BRANDON GREGORY JOSHUA WALSH
K-LOVE FILMS   WRITTEN BY JON ERWIN   IN THEATERS 2021   DIRECTED BY THE ERWIN BROTHERS   LIONSGATE